W9-BAF-219

THE Soul OF A Nation

James Robison

THOMAS NELSON
Since 1798

NASHVILLE · DALLAS · MEXICO CITY · RIO DE JANEIRO · BEIJING

Soul of a Nation

Copyright © 2008 by James Robison

Published in Nashville, Tennessee, by Thomas Nelson®, Inc.
Thomas Nelson is a registered trademark of Thomas Nelson, Inc.

Unless otherwise noted, all quotations are from the *New American Standard Bible*®. Copyright © The Lockman Foundation 1960, 1962, 1963, 1968, 1971, 1972, 1973, 1975, 1977, 1995. Used by permission.

Project Manager: Lisa Stillwell
Design: Koechel Peterson and Associates Inc., Minneapolis, MN

ISBN-10: 1-4041-0528-X
ISBN-13: 978-1-4041-0528-7

Printed and bound in China

www.thomasnelson.com

Table of Contents

INTRODUCTION

30 Days of Prayer for the Future of Our Nation

I BELIEVE we have reason to be deeply concerned about obvious trends in our nation. Over the last several decades, morality has spiraled downward into a relativistic, decadent attitude. The result: an American culture that devalues life, liberty, and essential goodness.

Forty years ago, if the ability to travel forward in time had been available, I think we would have been utterly astonished at how much America's values have changed. Consider the following:

The integrity of family as God originally created it is under attack because some believe that marriage is not exclusively between a man and a woman. Unborn babies, innocent and silent, are being slaughtered by the thousands in the name of personal freedom of choice. From Capitol Hill to the local barber shop, many cling to personal agendas and pride; our division compromises the peace and justice we should be ushering into the world. Apathy has too often replaced compassion, as people focus more on their own appetites than the needs of others.

Yes, we live in a different time and place than I knew growing up. But while I am heartbroken over the sin and evil that have encroached on this great nation, I am also encouraged. I am convinced that God has blessed America for more than two hundred years because He wants to use us as His agents of freedom and grace in this world.

There are still millions of believers in this country who have the supernatural power to turn the tide back to truth and light. Through prayer and obedient involvement in our neighborhoods, communities, and government, we *will* see positive change.

This book will take you through thirty days of my thoughts concerning the condition of America, followed by a parallel Scripture reading to help you gain God's perspective on these issues. But perhaps the most important parts of this book are the prayers at the end of each day's reading. I invite you to join me in interceding for the redemption and transformation of American thought.

I pray that as you diligently seek truth and hope in these pages, the Lord will enlighten and inspire you. Change will not come unless you and I, as lights in this world, get on our knees to seek the power we need to shine so brightly that this pervading darkness will finally be defeated. All that is necessary to dispel darkness is turning on the light.

One Nation Under God

LONG BEFORE George W. Bush named Jesus as his favorite philosopher, our founding fathers laid the foundation for this Christian nation, "one nation under God," which countless political leaders throughout our history have upheld.

The day our first president was inaugurated, George Washington said this in his address to Congress: ". . . it would be peculiarly improper to omit in this first official act, my fervent supplications to that Almighty Being, who rules over the universe, who presides in the council of nations, and whose providential aids can supply every human defect, that His benediction may consecrate to the liberties and happiness of the people of the United States."[1]

Patrick Henry clearly identified the underpinnings of American society when he said, "It cannot be emphasized too strongly or too often that this great nation was founded, not by religionists, but by

Christians; not on religions, but on the Gospel of Jesus Christ. For this very reason peoples of other faiths have been afforded asylum, prosperity, and freedom of worship here."[2]

This foundation of faith helped carry our country through the trials of the Civil War. President Abraham Lincoln issued a historic day of fasting and prayer on March 30, 1863. "And whereas, it is the duty of nations as well as of men to own their dependence upon the overruling power of God, to confess their sins and transgressions in humble sorrow yet with assured hope that genuine repentance will lead to mercy and pardon, and to recognize the sublime truth, announced in the Holy Scriptures and proven by all history: that those nations only are blessed whose God is the Lord."[3]

President Harry S. Truman, who made one of the most difficult moral decisions of our history when he dropped the atom bombs on Hiroshima and Nagasaki to end World War II, viewed our nation this way: "The fundamental basis of this nation's law was given to Moses on the Mount. The fundamental basis of our Bill of Rights comes from the teaching we get from Exodus and St. Matthew, from Isaiah and St. Paul. I don't think we emphasize that enough these days. If we don't have the proper fundamental moral background, we will finally end up with a totalitarian government which does not believe in the right for anybody except the state."[4]

In modern society, President Jimmy Carter encouraged, "We should live our lives as though Christ were coming this afternoon."[5]

Despite the overstated "separation of church and state" argument, numerous U.S. presidents have unapologetically woven God and Jesus Christ into their conversations, speeches, and memoirs.

Truly, America is the most Christian nation in modern history. I believe that this is why we are the most prosperous, liberated country in the world. This is also why we must accept and embrace our role as a world leader and adhere to the foundational principles that put us in this unique position to lead.

America needs leaders who will look beyond themselves to the Higher Power for wisdom and guidance. President Ronald Reagan said it best when he reminded us, "If we ever forget that we're one nation under God, then we will be a nation gone under. If I could just make a personal statement of my own—in these three-and-a-half years I have understood and known better than ever before the words of Lincoln, when he said that he would be the greatest fool on this footstool called Earth if he ever thought that for one moment he could perform the duties of that office without help from One who is stronger than all."[6]

Read Psalm 37.

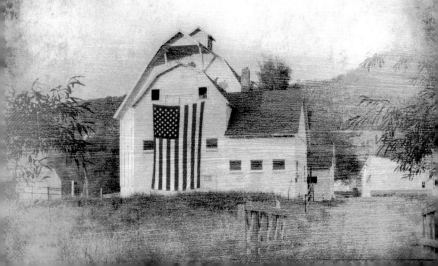

★★★ PRAYER ★★★

Father, the history of this nation demonstrates that You bless those who follow You. For more than two hundred years, You have placed men and women in leadership positions who know and fear You. You have consistently called out Your people to seek and serve You. And because of Your generous provision in godly leadership and godly citizens, You have also poured out Your goodness on us. Lord, though there is a trend in our society to reject You, we still love and honor You. Please turn the hearts of the strayed ones back to You and continue to bless our land.

Why Would God Bless America?

"GOD BLESS AMERICA!" It's a phrase we hear and see every-where: on bumper stickers, in songs, and at the close of speeches. But what are we saying with these words?

First, by addressing God, we personalize a request. We acknowl-edge a Creator, a Higher Power, a Divine Being. We rightly shatter the falsified wall that ignores a healthy division of church and state and strives to create a stridently secular nation. By asking God to do something, we recognize our human limitations and desperate need for supernatural intervention to guide us to liberty and pro-tect us from evil.

Second, we invoke an awesome action called "blessing." Jesus Christ, the greatest Teacher of life and love, once outlined the true meaning of blessing and revealed to us exactly who could receive it. The blessed are the poor in spirit, the gentle, the meek, the merci-ful, the peacemakers, and the pure in heart (Matthew 5:3–9).

Pride, arrogance, and self-righteousness cannot, by the pure nature of God, coexist with God's blessing.

Those who have a broken heart, who care for others, and who show mercy will find themselves in a position to receive God's blessing. Though we are imperfect, fallen creatures, we can still hunger and thirst for godly righteousness, cleanse our hearts and minds, and work for peace. In doing so, we allow God to pour out His blessing upon us.

It is important to understand that bringing justice to evildoers and protecting the innocent works in favor of peace. Pacifism merely allows chaos and tyranny to reign. Like a skilled surgeon aggressively pursuing a cancerous tumor, a just and righteous nation will remove the evil that seeks to destroy its people.

Our Teacher also said that we are blessed when we are persecuted or attacked for doing what is right (Matthew 5:11–12). As blessed individuals, Jesus compared us to light and salt, meaning that we

show the right way to live by our example. When we allow that light to shine, we become a bright city set on a hill by which the world can see the path to peace and prosperity (Matthew 5:13–16).

Logically, when we engage in attitudes and actions contrary to these principles, we remove ourselves from the possibility of blessing. If we are self-absorbed, uncaring, greedy, or deceitful, we cannot expect any divine favor.

Finally, when we ask this blessing upon America, or any nation, we seek something not merely for ourselves but for our fellow man. Before the ancient cities of Sodom and Gomorrah were destroyed, God promised Abraham that He would spare the impending doom if only ten righteous men could be found (Genesis 18:32). Though the vast majority of the people deserved anything but blessing, God was willing to extend it to the whole population on behalf of a small group.

We know that there will always be evil among us, even in our own communities, but the grace of God allows even a small group of us to request His blessing on everyone, if we will only position ourselves to receive it.

So when we say, "God bless America," let us understand the importance of our relationship with God, as well as our attitudes and actions toward other people. We should not dare utter it flippantly if we desire Him to respond to our request. It should be our earnest prayer and the desire we diligently seek.

Read Ezekiel 22:30.

★★★ PRAYER ★★★

*Lord, here I am, to stand in the gap for my land.
Thank You for placing so many of Your people around me
to pray for America; please help us to not give up the
opportunity to be a blessing on the country we love so
dearly. Truly, I ask for Your blessing over us. You alone are
capable of protecting us and guiding us in
righteousness. We desire Your goodness and
mercy above all, and I unashamedly ask
You to pour them lavishly upon us.
I do not ask this simply for myself or
even for my family, but for my neighbors
and countrymen, especially the ones who
do not know You. Have mercy on them.
Usher them into Your family. Make us a
Christian nation, not just by history,
but in hearts and actions as well.
Yes, God, bless us. Bless America.*

An Invitation to Pray

SINCE THE CONTINENTAL CONGRESS asked the colonies to pray for wisdom in forming a nation in 1775, the call to prayer has resounded throughout our history. President Lincoln officially proclaimed a day of "humiliation, fasting, and prayer" in 1863. In 1952, a joint resolution by Congress and signed by President Truman declared an annual National Day of Prayer. In 1988, the law was amended and signed by President Reagan, permanently setting the day as the first Thursday of every May.

President and Mrs. Bush honored my wife Betty and me by inviting us to come to the White House for the National Day of Prayer. Some in attendance expressed how honored they felt to be recognized by the highest office in our land and invited to pray. At the same time, it is important to grasp the fact that each of us has the greatest invitation possible from the highest authority in the universe. God Almighty, the most powerful force in existence, has invited us to come boldly into His presence through prayer.

Since He has extended this invitation and even commanded us to pray, we have to believe that it makes a difference when we do so.

Water that is concentrated through a turbine at a hydroelectric plant produces enough energy to light an entire city. I believe, in the same way, concentrated prayer releases a supernatural force that can, in the truest and purest sense, light up the world. A positive witness in a dark world stands out as clearly as a city set on a hill.

I am grateful we have a president who firmly believes in the importance and power of prayer, because it is only through prayer that positive change can come about.

As we pray, God can enlighten our hearts to the true understanding of peace, liberty, and freedom. Corporate peace only comes when individuals have first made peace with God and then seek peace with others. Liberty is far more than a social or political condition; it is the spiritual state of living. *Freedom is the ability to do what we should rather than the right to do what we want.* We need to see the world the way God sees the world.

Beyond changing our perspective, prayer moves God. He promises to hear us when we call on Him. He says, "Call to Me and I will answer you, and I will tell you great and mighty things" (Jeremiah 33:3), and if "My people who are called by My name humble themselves and pray and seek My face . . . then I will hear from heaven . . . and will heal their land" (2 Chronicles 7:14).

America and the rest of the world desperately need attention from Almighty God. We can intercede for them and see God do amazing things in our midst.

I am so thankful for how He has faithfully responded to our requests already. Terrorists have been captured, and enemies of freedom are being exposed and brought to justice. Beyond the threats that face our nation in this world, we must also realize there are terrorists in the spiritual realm seeking to destroy us. Greed, selfishness, and indifference toward the needs of others are examples of spiritual enemies that are just as damaging to our well-being as the terrorists.

The call to prayer is not a futile religious exercise. Prayer changes us and moves God. Our nation has never been in more need of change than it is today. We must respond to the evil and injustice around us by calling on the power of God to move on our behalf. Change begins when we get on our knees.

Read 1 Timothy 2:1–4.

★★★ PRAYER ★★★

Father, we desperately need Your intervention in this world. All around us evil pervades and threatens to overtake us. You are good and Your power is greater than any enemy we face. Give us Your eyes to see the circumstances as You see them. Give us Your heart of compassion to respond to our enemies with love. Grant our leaders wisdom as they guide us through wars, laws, and relationships with the rest of the world. Thank You for standing as the ultimate and sovereign authority. We trust You to establish peace and justice among us.

Changing the World for Good

WE ARE AT A CRITICAL TIME in the history of our country and our world. As America and our allies attempt to reshape the social and political landscape of the Middle East, we must define the standard by which we measure success.

How should we conduct ourselves as the major superpower on our planet? What are our objectives in places like Iraq, Palestine, and North Korea? Is our mission simply to create democracies, or is there a higher calling?

America has risen to the position of a leader among nations. As such, this nation should certainly be strong, very strong. However, it is critical that America also be good. The Soviet Union demonstrated how a powerful state without a moral compass is doomed to fail. But what do I mean by "good"?

Chester A. Pennington said, "No amount of good deeds can make us good persons. We must be good before we can do good."[1] Goodness is more than an act; it is a condition. Beyond the explanation of human philosophies, goodness transcends man's effort to define it. Goodness derives from One far greater than ourselves.

Often, prevalent evil is easier to recognize, which gives us a better understanding of its opposite. For example, some societies, both past and present, have elevated the state above the individual. Consequently, the needs of society are fulfilled at the expense of ordinary people—sweatshops abound, health care is an after-thought, and human rights are nonexistent. In other societies, religious fanaticism rules. Power is held by a select few, and many of the laws make little sense to the population. Women are treated poorly; independent thought is squashed; nonbelievers are punished or killed.

If indifference to the intrinsic value of people is so clearly seen as evil, then it is safe to say that goodness, the opposite of evil, places a high value on people. A "good" society esteems every person, whether tall or short, black or white, male or female, young or old, healthy or infirm, simple or intelligent, and so on. In a good society, people matter more than ideas, beliefs, or creeds.

Goodness defends individuals and their rights. Liberty is cherished, not in the sense of issuing license to do whatever one wishes, but in the stability to live within the self-imposed confines of a peaceful society. This is why we hail our members of the armed services as heroes. They are not conquering land for personal gain; they are eliminating evil oppressors so that we, and others, can live in peace.

As we seek to change other parts of the world for good, we must recognize the need for internal changes as well. Abuses and injustice still occur within our own borders, proving our need to reestablish fundamental goodness in our own society. We should be more concerned about being an example to the world than being its judge.

In our attempts to eradicate evil around the world, we must remain vigilant to ensure that we are serving a cause higher than ourselves. Our actions and motivations must be pure, or we will simply become crusaders for democracy, attempting to shape the rest of the world in our image. Historically, such strategies have failed miserably.

This world needs more goodness. But if we try to do good in the world before first becoming good ourselves, we will not succeed. First we must *be,* and then we can effectively *do*.

Read Proverbs 6:12–19 and Psalm 92:12–15.

★★★ PRAYER ★★★

Oh, God, the heart of man is wicked. Apart from You, no goodness is possible. Make me good from the inside out. Turn the heart of our nation from evil to righteousness. Allow us to spread Your justice and mercy throughout the earth. Convict our hearts of the sins we let rule over us and teach us how to submit only to Your lordship. Draw us close to You, so that out of our relationship with You, Your goodness can flow into the world around us.

A Seed of Suffering

SIMON WIESENTHAL LOST almost one hundred relatives in concentration camps during World War II. This so-called "Nazi hunter" later helped bring over eleven-hundred war criminals, captors, torturers, leaders, and murderers to face world courts. His past was marked by suffering, so he devoted his life to justice.

Clearly, the horrors of the Holocaust left a mark upon this man. If we could pinpoint one evil from the time that shaped his life, what would it be?

It's the same thing that continues to plague our world today. From the flooded streets of New Orleans to the blood-soaked sands of Iraq . . . in the scandalous lives of a church council president turned serial killer and a CEO greedily plundering the pensions of his employees . . . behind the genocides in Sudan and deep in the heart of every person on earth, past or present . . . the problem is the same: sin.

Sin is the seed rooted in every human at birth. It is a weed that, left untended, will choke out all semblance of goodness and decency. Sin germinates within the human soul, expressing itself in various forms. A seed of anger may sprout into hatred or even murder. A seed of selfishness may sprout into greed, deception, or thievery. A seed of lust can grow into moral compromise, betrayal, or rape.

Every form of human suffering can be traced back to sin. Divorce courts are filled with couples torn apart by the sin of infidelity. Prisons overflow with cheaters, swindlers, robbers, rapists, murderers, and child molesters. Graveyards collect the victims of gangs, racism, and brutality. War is always the result of someone's sin, either as an aggressor or oppressor.

Our government merely prunes the leaves of sin, cutting back extreme behavior, while leaving the infected stem intact. Churches, mental health professionals, and self-help groups dig deeper, unearthing core causes of sinful conduct in an attempt to eradicate the roots. While these approaches seem to be more effective in targeting the seed and not just the fruit, we continue to live in a world overgrown with the ugliness of sin.

It is not enough to simply treat the symptoms of sin or even to destroy its roots. Unless a new seed is planted, the old roots of evil will repeatedly fill empty spaces and grow stronger.

The apostle Paul referred to himself as chief among sinners (1 Timothy 1:15). Until he experienced a supernatural encounter with Jesus, he violently persecuted first-century Christians. When he met Jesus on the road to Damascus, a new seed was planted in his heart, empowering him to become "a new creature" (2 Corinthians 5:17). This remarkable transformation turned him from Christianity's primary enemy to its most influential evangelist, still impacting the world today.

Simon Wiesenthal said, "None of my 'clients'—not Eichmann, not Stangl, not Mengele, and not even Hitler or Stalin—was born a criminal. Somebody had to teach them to hate."[1] I disagree. The hatred was simply a preexisting seed of sin that flourished in these monsters' lives.

While Wiesenthal served society well by diligently working toward justice, mankind will never overcome the Nazis of the world until sin is torn out by the roots and replaced with a new seed, capable of producing good fruit.

The testimonies of those who have suffered at the hands of sinners should compel us to deal properly with the roots of sin, so that we will not continue to repeat the cycles of suffering and pain.

Read Romans 3:9–26.

★★★ PRAYER ★★★

Lord, I confess that there is nothing good in this fallen world apart from You. Thank You for transforming me, giving me a new nature that allows me to make a positive difference in this world. Give me Your eyes to see the evil around me for what it is: fruit of the sin rooted in every man's heart. Teach me how to confront sin with Your righteousness. Conquer the evil in this world and establish Your goodness in our midst. Have mercy on those suffering at the hands of sinful man and bring deliverance to the helpless. Use me as an instrument of grace in this fallen world.

Debating Moral Issues

MORAL ISSUES are continually at the forefront of political and social discussions in America. Euthanasia, pedophilia, violence, homosexuality, and abortion are just a few topics that dominate our conversation and deeply affect our lives.

We should be certain where we stand on these matters. Scripture is very clear when it comes to concerns of morality. However, as we face these issues with strong convictions, it is critical that we communicate our hearts with wisdom, love, and self-control. History's strongest moral leaders, from Jesus Christ to Gandhi, Martin Luther King, Jr. to Nelson Mandela, all stood up to the injustices of their times without resorting to any extremism.

Far too many moral activists, on both sides of the debate, seem to be more concerned with exterminating the opposition rather than establishing healthy moral standards. Their mean-spirited attitudes may stem from good intentions, but character assassination, militant rhetoric, and violence cannot be allowed to hijack our social and political debate.

No matter the moral topic, there are dangerous edges even on both ends of the opinion spectrum. The "intolerant" position demands rigid uniformity. Individuals must conform to their hard-line positions or be ostracized. Extremists will even turn against their advocates if they do not express their convictions zealously or forcefully enough.

At the other end of the spectrum, the "tolerant" movement insists there are no moral absolutes. Those who speak out against another's behavior, even peacefully, are mocked, labeled, and castigated.

Either of these extremes can lead to destruction. The debate must evolve into one tempered by wisdom and understanding. Beneficial communication can only occur between those who use discernment and compassion to discover balance and truth.

The poor decisions we make today impact the world our children and grandchildren will inherit from us. Like an earthquake, we see and feel the tremors caused by radicals on both sides. And like a tsunami, these choices quietly build upon one another until one day we find ourselves drowning in the consequences. Let there be no doubt: we reap what we sow.

There is an effective way for opposing sides to confront moral issues. The key lies in the approach. Proverbs 15:1 says, "A gentle

answer turns away wrath / But a harsh word stirs up anger."
Proverbs 25:15 says, "By forbearance a ruler may be persuaded /
And a soft tongue breaks the bone."

I have personally met with numerous influential clergy, politicians,
and business leaders and watched them reverse their positions on
moral issues. Having heard my sincere beliefs, communicated with
respect and love, they thoughtfully considered the challenges I
made to their line of reasoning and saw the truth behind them. I
also arranged meetings with opponents who have been taught to
fear one another to the point of being unable to hear each other
clearly. Hateful arrogance toward one's adversary gets you nowhere.

While silence is certainly deadly, bitter zeal can be even more damaging in its polarization. Attitudes and actions speak louder than
words. Truth will withstand debate, but only when it is communicated in love!

We need a new birth of patient and considerate reasoning, leading
to rational decisions that more effectively promote and protect
godly morality. When emotions run high, some will stampede
blindly down the broad way of destruction. Those of us who
receive the counsel of Scripture must set the example of treading
upon the narrow path to life. It is the light of love which will ultimately reveal the way.

Read Ecclesiastes 10:11–15 and Colossians 4:5–6.

★★★ PRAYER ★★★

Lord, open our eyes to the schemes of Satan. When he attempts to divide us with arguments, pride, and misunderstanding, give us humility to consider others better than ourselves. Teach us how to hold fast to Your standards of morality while still communicating truth with grace and love. Give us the meekness we need in order to learn from others. Exalt us in the eyes of our opponents so that they might see Your truth and embrace Your ways.

Illegal Immigration: A Humanitarian Crisis

DESPITE CURRENT RHETORIC, the flow of millions of illegal workers to this country has not yet created an economic crisis, a political crisis, or a national security crisis. It has, however, created a moral crisis.

I've said it hundreds of times, and I will continue to say it: people matter most. Right now, millions are suffering, and that is not a status quo we should settle for.

Every summer, in Texas and other border states, migrants from Latin America die horrible deaths. While crossing barren land, they fall victim to dehydration or fatigue. They suffocate in the backs of packed trailers and railroad cars.

Yet, even in the face of life-threatening situations, they still come by the millions. Why? Two reasons: their own countries encourage them to leave, and we encourage them to come.

The primary reason we have an illegal immigration problem is the corruption and mismanagement within the governments of Mexico, Nicaragua, El Salvador, Colombia, and other countries south of the border. The income gap between the United States and Mexico is the largest between any two adjacent countries in the world, according to Stanford historian David Kennedy.[1]

Of course people want to come to the United States. Who would blame them?

The motivation for allowing undocumented aliens into our country ranges from corruption to compassion. Politicians turn a blind eye to the situation to avoid losing votes from the Hispanic community. Social activists and labor unions exploit the situation for their own personal gain as well. Many greedy companies benefit from cheap labor, maximizing their profits by minimizing the ethical treatment of their employees.

Paradoxically, the goodness of average Americans contributes to the problem. We like to give people in need an opportunity to succeed, and we know that the vast majority of those coming are decent, hard workers who are simply trying to learn valuable trades and improve their families' lives.

What we all seem to miss is the fact that the current climate constitutes a moral crisis of the highest order. Families are torn apart as able-bodied men leave their wives and children, some never to return. Communities in the poorest regions of Latin America spiral into deeper poverty as the talented and dedicated laborers go north. Human traffickers, known as "coyotes," reap the benefits of smuggling people across the border, often extorting shameful amounts of money from their "cargo." Migrants passing through Mexico are robbed, beaten, and raped by bandits and even police. Hospitals along the border shut down under the burden of poor, uninsured patients, leaving everyone without adequate medical care.

Illegal immigration will continue to be a problem as long as the economic and political conditions in the United States are drastically better than those in neighboring countries. Few benefit from the current status quo. Long-term good for the whole population will only come when we reform our immigration laws to provide a clear pathway to citizenship, secure the borders, and pressure failed governments to eradicate corruption and pursue aggressive economic policies.

The saying goes that good intentions pave the road to hell. Too many poor, desperate Latinos travel that road. Without reform, the human rights of millions will continue to be routinely violated. For the sake of those without a voice—either in their home countries or in the United States—we must pursue a humane policy of immigration and regional development. This is the right path because it is right for people.

Read Matthew 14:13–21.

★★★ PRAYER ★★★

Oh Father, You are full of compassion and love. People are the treasures of Your creation, and You love them completely. Thank You for seeing every person even in their trial and tribulation. There is no circumstance too difficult for You to handle. Show us the right path of wisdom and love for our neighbors. Give our leaders discernment as they set laws and regulations that can be a path of life for those who are oppressed and hopeless. Protect the children who are victims of the societies they are born into and of the decisions their parents make. Allow us to be Your hands of justice and compassion.

Defending the Indefensible

A PREGNANT WOMAN in New York drank so much vodka during her last trimester that her baby was born drunk. She was charged with child endangerment.

A Hawaiian woman consumed so much speed that her newborn son died two days after his birth. She was charged with manslaughter.

In California, a woman was sentenced to life in prison for poisoning her infant through her breast milk tainted with methamphetamines.

What do all three cases have in common? Each of these women, as well as others accused of harming their fetuses, have one leading advocate: the National Organization for Women (NOW). In addition to their defense lawyers, these women are supported by this powerful organization that uses their cases to promote and protect their own agenda.

An article in *Newsweek* revealed that this far-left sociopolitical group has "cranked up its campaign" against such cases against women because of their fear that it could open the door to legal grounds for "fetal personhood"—the idea that a child in the womb is actually a human being and not just a mass of tissue.[1]

Despite the advances in modern medicine and prenatal understanding, NOW and others in our society are blinded by a decades-old allegiance to the landmark *Roe v. Wade* case legalizing abortion. In 1973, mothers could not watch their third-trimester infants suck their thumbs, turn their heads, and even smile in the womb. When my forty-year-old mother conceived me out of a forced sexual relationship, she did not have the ability to view me via an ultrasound or even hear my heartbeat. Because of her situation, she did not need a child, so she sought an abortion. Fortunately for me, her doctor refused to perform it or refer her elsewhere.

The thought that anyone could promote the protection of personal ideology over human life illustrates the lack of moral guidance in much of society. Such a blind allegiance is akin to the superstitions of the Aztec mothers that persuaded them to offer up their children as sacrifices to the gods. The modern God of ideological idolatry now accepts these child sacrifices in order to protect certain women's "right to choose."

The truth is, these cases poignantly illustrate the problem with today's abortion argument that an unborn child is a nonperson. When my wife discovered she was pregnant, she did not announce, "I'm going to have a fetus!" She, like every other woman entering the joys of motherhood, exclaimed, "I'm going to have a baby!"

Since science has come to some level of agreement as to when life ends (generally accepted as the cessation of brain activity), we should at least put the same medical and political effort into determining when life begins. Then we increase our chances to agree that every life is precious and worth defending. Though many may never agree because they continue to bow to their false gods, we should at least establish a foundation upon which to build. The "fetal personhood" debate needs to return to common sense.

Read Psalm 139:13–18.

★★★ PRAYER ★★★

Father, You are the masterful Creator, the only One capable of knitting together and forming the human body and soul after Your image. I recognize Your hand in the conception and growth of babies in the womb, and I agree with You that all life is valuable. Forgive us as a nation for not esteeming the worth of unborn babies. Have mercy on us for the millions of murders that have occurred since 1973. For the sake of the innocent victims unable to stand up for themselves and for Your name's sake, bring a civil end to legalized abortion. Bring about change in the hearts of the American people to see and value the lives of human beings at conception. Give us Your eyes and equip us with Your wisdom and power that we might see and protect the futures of these children.

The Path to Peace

IT HAS BEEN SAID that if we do not learn from history, we are doomed to repeat it. But there is one historical pattern that we would be wise to learn from: national forgiveness.

Nations typically evolve from friction. The United States was born out of a revolution. Canada pulled away from colonial rule. Mexico fought for independence from Spain. But each of these countries, over time, sought reconciliation with their former enemies.

Before reconciliation is possible, forgiveness must be extended. Only after a genuine purge of resentment and bitterness can two groups of people restore peaceful relations.

Within a single generation, conquered Germany became our friend, largely because the Allies extended grace and forgiveness to the good people of the former Nazi regime, even while pursuing justice.

Even Japan, which suffered a tremendous loss of honor and human life as the target of the only atomic bombs ever dropped, quickly became a true ally to the United States, Britain, Australia, and other one-time enemies. Though many Japanese citizens still bear the physical scars of their national nightmare, forgiveness enabled emotional healing on a nationwide level. While never forgetting the shock and pain of Pearl Harbor, the United States has not only forgiven Japan but also supports their technology and craftsmanship through the free market.

Perhaps the most poignant illustration of modern-day forgiveness and reconciliation lies in the racial, religious, and class divides that nearly ripped apart the nation of South Africa. Apartheid crushed a bloody tribal territory with the heavy boot of oppression, which then gave rise to a people's revolution that witnessed atrocities committed not by just one or two sides but by three. The ruling white party, Nelson Mandela's freedom fighters, and the Zulu nation engaged in guerrilla warfare for years before they finally constructed a framework for peace. Today, overall stability prevails because all three parties agreed to forgive the aggression of the past and work together for the peace of the future.

My missionary partner in Africa, Peter Pretorius, said that it was only through forgiveness that his country was spared an all-out, multipartied civil war. F. W. DeKlerk, Nelson Mandela, and Chief Buthelezi set the example for forgiveness and brought about the reconciliation of what is arguably the strongest country on the continent of Africa.

Once again, our world faces a future yearning for forgiveness. In Iraq, the Kurds, Sunni, and Shia must learn the concept of nationwide forgiveness. Certainly vengeance seems justified in some cases, but it must be replaced with a justice system that remedies the need for mob action or vigilantism.

Israel and Palestine must find a way to forgive each other for so many years of war and death. Otherwise there will be no end to their pain and the instability that plagues the region. Each side radically defends its position due to the enormous grief they have endured, but choosing sides will not bring forgiveness or peace.

The Muslim doctrine of murder and vengeance must be exchanged for divine reconciliation with the understanding that we are all guilty of injuring another. If we are to be judged and sentenced for our offenses, then we are all guilty and deserve payback.

Our nation must make reconciliation with past and present enemies a priority. And the first step toward that reconciliation is forgiveness. Without forgiveness, there is no hope for a peaceful future.

Read John 20:19–23.

★★★ PRAYER ★★★

God, it is awesome to look back through history and see how our nation and others have benefited from forgiveness. You modeled forgiveness for us when You sent Jesus, and You remain true to the promises of blessing when we choose forgiveness as You did. The turmoil that rages throughout the Middle East needs healing, Lord. The people there hate each other, and they hate the rest of the world. They sulk as victims and justify retaliation. Bitterness and anger have hardened their hearts. Father, You are the healer of hurting hearts. Bring Your healing to that region in the form of forgiveness. Have mercy on them and teach them to have mercy on one another.

Kingdoms in Conflict

"CHARLES ROBERTS was not an evil person," the Reverend Robert Schenck told CNN.[1] Roberts reportedly dreamed of molesting young children, but instead he walked into an Amish schoolroom, bound and shot little girls execution-style, then turned the gun on himself. Anyone doubting evil exists must acknowledge that for those few hellish moments, it manifested in that one-room Pennsylvania school.

Marie Roberts, Charles's widow, released the following statement:

> The man that did this today was not the Charlie
> I've been married to for almost ten years. My
> husband was loving, supportive, and thoughtful. . . .
> He was an exceptional father. He took the kids to
> soccer practice and games, played ball
> in the backyard, and took our seven-year-old
> daughter shopping.[2]

According to the person who knew him best, Charlie sounded normal. Despite the last hour of his life, this man does not appear to have been a monster. He seemed to spend his life changing diapers and playing with his kids, not plotting malevolent acts.

There is a conflict here. Something doesn't add up. How can a seemingly normal man commit such hideous acts? Is mankind so depraved that we are all capable of the worst atrocities? Do we all live on the verge of a physical or psychological imbalance that could, without warning, thrust us into a Jekyll-and-Hyde rage?

The evidence recorded in humanity's catalog of crimes suggests a universal struggle between darkness and light—two kingdoms warring for the souls of men. We see the manifestation of these two kingdoms in the news every day. The media tends to focus on the darkness: suicide bombers in the Middle East, genocide in Sudan, a bomb-building dictator in North Korea, and a rash of school shootings in the United States. The kingdom of light gets less attention, but every testimony gives us hope: a firefighter rescuing a child, a scientist conquering a disease, and a missionary delivering food to starving people.

The kingdoms of light and darkness clash in a conflict over the souls of men. Whether we realize it or not, decisions we make daily further the cause of one kingdom or the other. Bob Dylan summed it up when he sang, "It may be the devil or it may be the Lord, but you're gonna have to serve somebody."[3]

The influence of the invisible realm on the visible is undeniable. A battle rages both within the human heart and in the outworking of our hearts in relationship to one another. In families and communities and between nations, good and evil wrestle for victory.

Those of us in the kingdom of light must understand that this spiritual battle with evil forces can only be fought with spiritual weapons. The virtues of love, compassion, courage, strength of character, and harmony of heart overcome the kingdom of darkness. These values must reign in our personal lives in order to advance the kingdom of light.

Too many people live on the edge of darkness, even those who appear to be average. Normal fathers, mothers, and children could be a few bad decisions away from becoming the next Charles Roberts. Our only hope is to turn to Jesus, the One who said, "I am the light of the world" (John 8:12). We need His supernatural strength to win this fight.

Good will ultimately triumph over evil, but meanwhile each of us must commit ourselves to the positive influence and power found only in the kingdom of light.

Read John 3:16–21.

★★★ PRAYER ★★★

Dear Jesus, You are a mighty warrior. Your compelling light conquers every evil force of darkness. The battle between good and evil, between You and Satan, that persists in the spiritual realm around me every moment seems daunting. Everywhere I turn, there seems to be more evidence of darkness than of light. And yet I know that You are the ultimate conqueror. I want to fight alongside You because I know You will win. Arm me with the virtues of love, compassion, courage, and character so that I can contend for the kingdom of light. Remove any discouragement or doubt from my mind when I see darkness manifest before me. Help me to respond with the light I have from You.

Loving Our Enemies

AFTER 9/11, a *New York Times* reporter asked me, "How do we respond to such blatant attacks?"

I replied that we must resist and overcome the enemy by fighting on two fronts: first, with the strongest military in human history, both defensively and offensively. We cannot allow the enemies of freedom to triumph over us.

Second, we should overcome forces of evil with the greatest release of love in human history. The reporter seemed confused. To her, these tactics stood in opposition to each other.

"It is not a contradiction," I explained. "We have an opportunity now, and we will have even more in the future. There are multitudes throughout the world, especially in developing countries, who need a friend—someone to care. America must show that we are not interested in exploiting other people's resources, but rather in helping develop the greatest resource: people. We must look for opportunities to extend our hands and open our hearts to help improve their lives. Our government, our businesses, and our individual citizens must seek ways to demonstrate the goodness of America to the hurting people of the world."

The reports that poured in following the devastating 6.3-magnitude earthquake that killed more than thirty thousand Iranians in December of 2003 were encouraging testimonies of proactive love. Who would have imagined that Iran, referred to as part of the "Axis of Evil," would welcome a helping hand from America, often referred to as the "Great Satan"!

On the short list of America's enemy states, Iran would certainly rank in the top five, challenging North Korea for the top spot. But Jesus said, "Love your enemies" (Matthew 5:44), and America chose to demonstrate love for the people of a nation perceived as an enemy. The enormity of this gesture should not be underestimated. If ever there was a "right thing" to do, this was it.

One of the first groups to reach the ruinous city of Bam, Iran, came from Alabama. Iranian helpers saw the words *Alabama Disaster Relief* stenciled on the side of supply crates and read it as *Ala,* similar to their word for God; *Ba,* their word for *with* and *ma,* meaning *us.* The Iranians translated *Alabama Disaster Relief* to mean "God-with-us Disaster Relief." The impression of Americans bringing God to their aid speaks louder than any speech, commentary, or treaty. It is life and love undeniable.

America should pursue such opportunities. Everywhere we see people suffering, we must strive to alleviate the pain. Throughout the last century, this has been one of the most powerful characteristics of our nation. Indeed, compassion could be the greatest weapon in our arsenal, because it so effectively encourages peace.

In the coming days and months, we will have many opportunities to love our enemies. While we can never embrace policies or actions that suppress the life and liberty of individuals, we can love those with whom we disagree. We can look for opportunities to bless the people who curse us, as the Bible instructs (Matthew 5:44).

Compassion works. It does not always happen overnight, but ultimately love conquers all.

Read Matthew 5:38–48.

★★★ PRAYER ★★★

Lord Jesus, Your standards for us are high. The world teaches us to hate and destroy our enemies, but You say to love them, bless them, and pray for them. This is so counter to what our hearts tell us to do. Remake our hearts, Lord. Give us Your heart so that we can move with love toward those who hate us. As You give us strength and opportunity to bless them, change their hearts toward us as well. Bring peace where there is hostility, unity where there is division. I do pray for our enemies, Lord. You see the anger and bitterness in their hearts. Reveal Your love to them and bring Your transforming healing. You alone are able to make something good tomorrow out of the evil that pervades today.

Defeating Darkness

"FOR WE MUST CONSIDER that we shall be as a City upon a hill. The eyes of all people are upon us." John Winthrop, the governor of the Massachusetts Bay Colony, wrote these words about one of our founding settlements nearly four hundred years ago.[1] Since that time, America has, for the most part, maintained faith in a guiding Light and shone the light of truth and freedom around the world.

Once again, the "eyes of all people" watch America to see if we will continue to be that light, even in the face of the greatest darkness on earth. Never has the hill upon which we sit been so visible.

In recent history, darkness has encroached upon truth and freedom: darkness under Hitler and Mussolini and darkness under the Soviet Union. Now we face the darkness under the radical, fascist regimes of Islamism, the political side of the Islamic religion that attempts to control the state, run society, and remake the human being.

Darkness *cannot* overcome light. There may be setbacks or distorted perceptions, but the fact of the matter remains—light will always triumph over darkness. In fact, there are only two circumstances in which darkness will ever be allowed to prevail. Americans and free people all over the world need to hear and know what these two scenarios are.

First, darkness will win in the absence of light. If you venture deep into the ocean or far below the earth, you can experience pitch black. No light means total darkness. The result is complete disorientation. There is no sense of space or direction. Any human left in these conditions would descend from immediate fear to almost certain insanity and death.

Second, darkness can reign as long as light is hidden. A full moon will cast no shadows on a cloudy night because its light is obscured. A lamp concealed by a basket fails to give light to the house. The same is true with the light of truth.

I don't believe that the world will experience pitch black as long as God's people occupy the earth. Certainly regions can fall into utter darkness, as evidenced by pervasive fear, insanity, and death, but the hope of truth and freedom still exists. The real danger exists when truth and freedom are hidden.

One of America's greatest strengths is freedom of thought. President John F. Kennedy said, "We are not afraid to entrust the American people with unpleasant facts, foreign ideas, alien philosophies, and competitive values. For a nation that is afraid to let its people judge the truth and falsehood in an open market is a nation that is afraid of its people."[2]

Truth withstands debate because light dispels darkness. The Islamists who seek to conquer nations forbid debate under the guise of Shari'a, or religious law. They attempt to subvert freedom of thought by suppressing freedom of expression. This darkness cannot be completely destroyed, but it can be pushed back as we shine the light of freedom and truth into the deepest corners of civilization.

This is the calling of America and all free people. We are a city set on a hill. The enemy sees our darkness and exploits it for their own purposes. We must shine truth brightly enough that all deception, fear, and oppression can be dispelled. In this, we must not fail.

The whole world is watching.

Read John 12:35–36, 46.

★★★ PRAYER ★★★

Jesus, You are the light of the world. Darkness cannot prevail in Your presence. I believe that You are the only hope for those oppressed by darkness. Shine Your love, truth, peace, and grace upon them so that they can receive the freedom You came to give. Allow those of us who know and follow You to reflect Your light. You commanded us to shine our light before men so that we will glorify the Father. Help us to shine brightly. Bring honor to Yourself by eliminating the overshadowing darkness in the world.

Destroying Division Through Dialogue

CONVERSATION HAS BEEN CALLED "a lost art." Despite an endless amount of talk nowadays, there seems to be an absence of real dialogue. However, one attempt at productive conversation caught my attention, and I believe it is worth noting.

In 2006, President Bush went to Asia to bolster China's relationship with the free world while urging the communist leaders to allow more economic and religious freedom. China's progress, Bush asserted, would not be jeopardized by more freedom; it would be enhanced. He also boldly emphasized the importance of democracy as one of freedom's greatest expressions and privileges.

Some would call this type of conversation a compromise. Others would say it is dangerous. But America must not be afraid to openly debate ideas, even with perceived enemies. Refusal to dialogue could prove to be the greatest compromise of all.

Too often, people build walls, and many times they erroneously support division with religious conviction. Jesus, the founder of Christianity, prayed that there would be oneness among His followers: unity with God and one another and, ultimately, a harmony of heart (John 17). Jesus also emphasized the importance of caring for and even loving our enemies. This does not take from governments the responsibility of providing protection for the innocent and dealing justice to the perpetrators of evil. It does, however, challenge us to seek every possible way to clear the lines of communication so that we can overcome spiritual and ideological chasms.

As a Baptist evangelist, I have been taught (as many other Protestant evangelicals have) that the Catholic Church falls short of "real" Christianity. While American Protestants and Catholics do not war outright, we have been trained to criticize or, at the very least, avoid one another. But Protestants and Catholics should not be enemies. We are, as Boston College professor of philosophy Peter Kreeft so eloquently points out, "separated brethren." He went on to say that we have addressed our disagreements "by consigning each others' bodies to graves on our battlefields, and each others' souls to hell."[1]

What a shame that professing Christians act in such Christ-less ways. By refusing to see those who disagree with them, the perpetrators are actually blinding themselves to the true teachings and path of Jesus, the One they claim is the way to God the Father.

This separation extends to all of mankind. East is separated from West. Muslim is separated from Jew. Black is separated from White. Democrat is separated from Republican. People have fought and died over such divisions.

It is time we begin living for constructive unity without compromising proven principles. The abandonment of forgiveness, open and honest dialogue, and the pursuit of healthy unity has been costly to all parties. Agreement should not be viewed simply as a relationship void of any differences. Differences do not dispel unity; selfishness does. It is this division that must be destroyed through dialogue dedicated to peace, truth, and healing.

America has always been a melting pot of races, religions, and creeds. At her finest moments, she has risen against the evils of the world, liberating the oppressed from tyrants and sharing her wealth with those in need. It is only when selfishness or corruption creeps into her heart that America becomes perverse and weak. If America will remain a bright light in history, principled unity must always remain her glorious pursuit.

Read Romans 12:9–21.

★★★ PRAYER ★★★

Father, I recognize the plot of Satan to bring discord where there should be unity. I ask You to teach me how to be a person of peace and harmony for the sake of Your kingdom. Unify Your church on the earth, breaking down walls of division between denominations, so that we can stand together to work for Your purposes on the earth. Open our eyes to where Satan seeks to divide us. Help us to walk in humility, putting aside selfish ambition for the sake of those in need. Help us to see and embrace Your goodness and truth in those we encounter. By Your grace, show us how to love our enemies.

Exposing the Real Enemy

AS CONSERVATIVES AND CHRISTIANS continue to rally around numerous social and political issues, it becomes more apparent that we are in a serious war. But do we really know which enemy we should be fighting?

Many decry the pollution of public airwaves with prime-time content that would have shocked past generations. But television networks are not the enemy.

High divorce rates fragment families, undermining one of the strongest foundations of civilization. But divorcées are not the enemy.

Abortion on demand still claims the lives of countless defenseless babies. But doctors who have spurned the Hippocratic Oath are not the enemy.

Sex crimes and pedophilia seem to be skyrocketing in an era when the Internet makes it easier than ever to prey upon children. But technology and people who abuse it are not the enemy.

Violence has become commonplace, even in our schools. But guns are not the enemy.

All over the country, voters are determining whether to reinforce the institution of marriage as one man and one woman in response to the agenda of gay activists who wish to impose their lifestyle as the norm. But homosexuals are not the enemy.

Radical Muslim malcontents riot from Paris to Jakarta, destroying property and wreaking havoc. But Muslims are not the enemy.

Terrorists continue to wage a guerrilla war in Iraq. Foreign fighters still infiltrate the ranks of the resistance. The good people of Iraq and the military coalition supporting them suffer losses every day. But terrorists are not the enemy.

There is one underlying force behind all of these tragedies, one source of everything that comes to kill, steal, and destroy. This force can take an inanimate object, like a computer or a box cutter, and turn it into a weapon of destruction. This force can also take people, like innocent children or priests, and turn them into monsters.

This force is rightly called evil.

Evil is a spiritual cancer that assaults all of mankind, struggling against conscience and reason to influence and even take control of our free will. In a world that often seems out of control, the truth is that many things are indeed under control—under the control of evil.

The only way to combat evil is to first recognize that it exists. There are those who try to convince us that everything is relative and that one man's evil is another man's good. This notion foolishly asks us to put on a blindfold before stepping onto a battlefield.

Others spend their time railing against the symptoms of evil without recognizing its root. While these people's causes often appear noble, their efforts amount to a cough drop fighting against a cold. It may make some people feel better about themselves, but the underlying virus still thrives.

Since evil is a powerful but invisible force influencing mankind's thoughts and actions, we must realize that it can only be detected, deterred, and defeated by supernatural power. We cannot ignore its existence, but we also cannot expect to defeat it on our own.

Darkness can only be dispelled by light; therefore, evil's deceptive deeds of destruction must be exposed by absolute, liberating Truth. Only when we receive the light of Truth can we begin to win the war against evil and its perpetrators.

Read Ephesians 6:10–20.

★★★ PRAYER ★★★

Lord, Your Word tells us that we are in a battle against an enemy we cannot see with our eyes. We confess our weakness and inability to fight and win such a war. But we also confess our faith in You to conquer the evil that seeks to destroy. Clothe us with Your armor of truth, righteousness, peace, faith, salvation, and Your Word. Teach us how to fight through prayer. Be our front and rear guard. As children of Your light, allow us to dispel the darkness around us. Keep us from fear; give us boldness for Your kingdom.

Going the Distance

ON JANUARY 9, 2003, thirty-one-year-old Staff Sergeant Mike McNaughton, a husband and father of five, stepped on an anti-personnel mine while serving in Afghanistan. The resulting blast cost him his right leg as well as the middle and ring fingers of his right hand and a chunk of his left leg. He was evacuated to Landstruhl Regional Medical Center in Germany for immediate treatment and later flown to Walter Reed Army Medical Center in Washington, D.C., for additional care.

While the sergeant was recuperating at Walter Reed, President Bush visited him. During the course of their conversation, they discussed their mutual enjoyment of jogging, and the president invited Sgt. McNaughton to go running with him once he was able.

After months of rehabilitation, McNaughton gained enough strength and mobility to take up the president's offer. The two jogged around the running track that encircles the White House's south lawn before rain forced them inside. They continued their workout in the White House gym, lifting weights and talking about McNaughton's recovery.

In a quote attributed to Baton Rouge television station WAFB, Sgt. McNaughton said, "We tried different [weight] equipment. He said I couldn't do it, so I had to prove him wrong. This goes back to my military training. I never once stopped something and said, 'I can't do it,' or quit just because I lost my leg. Why should I start now?"[1]

Sgt. McNaughton's attitude illustrates the courage and determination necessary for the United States, as well as every other country that cherishes freedom, to finish this war on terror. While it would have been easy for McNaughton to complain or find fault with some aspect of the operation in Afghanistan, he chose instead to overcome his setback and then honor his leader—and his whole country—with a few laps around the track.

Certainly a few sharp words would have gained McNaughton much more airtime and media coverage than his heroic recovery, but his attitude was not self-centered, critical, or embittered. (It is interesting to note that this story was buried outside of McNaughton's home state of Louisiana. Other than in the *New Orleans Times Picayune*, we could not find a major newspaper that reported this account. On the other hand, all current or former military personnel who criticize the president or the war seem to find themselves on half a dozen magazine covers or television news shows.)

McNaughton knew the risks of going into the war. He accepted them and paid a price far steeper than most of us. His tenacity and courage gave him the strength to bounce back time and time again. Sgt. McNaughton is now stronger than ever . . . if not in body, then certainly in spirit.

America is in a proactive recovery mode. Our wounds are still tender, but we are healing fast. At the same time, we are taking bold steps to become even stronger and more secure. Like Sgt. McNaughton's experience, our recuperation process involves discomfort and pain at times. But if we are ever going to take freedom's victory lap, we must put aside all grumbling and focus on overcoming the evil that threatens us.

Read 2 Timothy 2:3–6.

★★★ PRAYER ★★★

Thank You, Lord, for the faithful men and women who put their lives on the line day and night to protect my freedom and to ensure liberty for the oppressed. Protect them, Father, as they selflessly serve others. Help us, as a nation, not to dishonor their sacrifice by complaining about trials or running from the battle. Give our leaders wisdom in navigating this war on terror. Sustain us on the weary days of seeming defeat or devastating loss. Keep our eyes focused on where You are taking us. Establish peace in our midst. Though many of us are not on the actual battlefield, allow us to take part in Your work in this world. Keep us from sin and evil so we will not be disqualified from Your service. Show us how we can do our part in overcoming the evil in this world.

We Have a Choice: Humility or Humiliation

For several years I have sensed in my spirit some awesome and alarming things when I meditate on the Scriptures and pray. I have waited a long time, but I believe the time has come for me to finally share these impressions.

I earnestly pray that the free world and especially America—my home and the land of the free, where many choose to live as slaves bound by appetites and actions, demanding their way rather than God's way—may somehow be spared the horrendous results such decadent practices have produced throughout history. **I don't want us to get what we deserve.**

I cry out for mercy for me, my family members, and everyone— even those who choose to be our enemies. I don't want anyone to perish but all to repent, just as the Bible expresses. This is the very desire of God's heart. Please join me in focused prayer.

I am convinced that brokenness will come to the church and to America. The choice is ours: **humility or humiliation!** Our population will cry out to God, on our faces, desperate beyond comprehension, in unity of spirit and heart, longing for what really matters. The whole world will long for peace—not just national or world peace, but God's peace within thier hearts and lives. It's not peace as the world gives, having everything our way, but rather having it His way, having what only Jesus can give. People, not material things, will matter most. Our focus will be on love, relationships, family, joy, compassion, and serving others.

Those who claim no faith will respectfully acknowledge the importance of our First Amendment guarantees. They will be accorded the same respect from the faith community. Open dialogue, debate, and difference will no longer be rooted in a desire to destroy opposition.

Brokenness Will Lead to True Character

A change of heart and direction will take place in this nation. Brokenness will lead to true character, determination, self-sacrifice, and a sincere desire to know and do what is right, regardless of the cost or sacrifice. The line distinguishing good and evil will be as distinct as the difference between light and darkness—the difference being as clear to all observers as the difference between terrorists flying airplanes into towers, killing unsuspecting people of all nations and races, and those brave souls risking their own lives, seeking to rescue them. The difference will be as distinct as suicide bombers killing innocent schoolchildren and the compassionate doctors and relief workers who strive to ease suffering around the world. There is the force of evil on one side and life-enriching righteousness on the other. We cannot continue to deny that evil is a reality, to tolerate and even defend it as a mere difference of opinion.

What I Share Next Is Sobering

I have resisted sharing what I believe I've seen in the Spirit, not because I doubt the accuracy, but because I long and pray that what I see will be averted. I pray for a change of heart and direction, for true repentance to occur until our nation as a whole receives the truth of God, begins to live with the character, strength, and faith that made America great in the first place, and allows selfless love rather than selfish indulgence to prevail.

As I said, I am convinced brokenness will come. Count on it. The Bible says God's Word is a hammer; its power can break our stubborn will. His Word is a fire; it can purify us. His Word is water; it can cleanse. The choice is ours: choose life or choose the way that seems right to men and women—the fruit of which is death.

We Must Witness the Change of Heart

If the current practice of abortion on demand, destroying the most helpless and innocent of human life, continues with bold, open approval, we will find all innocent life vulnerable to what has become a culture of death. How can we possibly expect our lives and our rights to be protected when we fail to offer basic protection to the most precious little ones? We must witness far more than the changing of any court's decision—we must witness the change of heart that will no longer terminate innocent life, however foolish some judge or legislator may be. Rest assured, our laws reflect the condition of our hearts.

We have made such an idol of economic gain and material possessions, I am not certain brokenness will come apart from the collapse of our economy and the loss of treasured possessions. Selfish indulgences, revealed through sexual excesses and perversion, are promoted and defended as perfectly acceptable and normal.

This attitude must be changed from within, and its effect will be visibly manifested in the lives and practices of our general population.

It's my hope that the church family will pray, seek God, turn from any wicked ways, and see our land healed. I pray that all unbelievers will respond to God's offer of life, forgiveness, and grace, resulting in supernatural intervention and protection. God is described in the Bible as "a mighty fortress," "the shields of the earth," "our Deliverer," and "the solid rock." The intentions of evildoers can be supernaturally detected and thwarted. The enemy must be changed or defeated.

We must have God's power and protection in order to miss our enemies' plan for us. Without this divine miracle, unparalleled, indescribable devastation is coming to our shores—truly "the sum of all fears."

I'm not referring to the natural disasters we are already witnessing and the challenges that reveal our nation's soul and character. I'm talking about deliberate destruction by the deadly actions of evil men.

Where Was God When This Happened?

Many times in prayer, I have seen agonizing pain and suffering resulting from a direct nuclear or biological strike in major population centers in the United States. I have seen masses of people crying out in fear and panic from destruction and death beyond comprehension. There is a cry for help and mercy, for a way of escape, for protection, for communication, for news of loved ones. Comfort is totally disrupted. A sense of total loss jeopardizes our way of life. Prayer is prevalent. People are desperate for help—even divine intervention. No one asks, "Is there a God?" It seems everyone is looking for Him, including those who once moved to keep God out of public life. Many ask, "Why?" Others ask, "Where was God when this happened?"

But people are not questioning the faith *of* others. They are looking for faith *in* others. I see brokenness and humility, along with humiliation, as those who once thought they stood firm, rapidly fall. Many high towers crumble. Households and communities tremble in the aftermath. Our way of life pales compared to the simple desire for life itself.

The only strength and hope for the future comes from those who are truly strong in the Lord. The most courageous prove to be the most compassionate; they understand pure love and willingly make sacrifices on behalf of others. Their genuine strength of character is revealed, and people wholeheartedly seek to hear God's truth. They want someone to provide clear direction, inspire proper action, and promise a stable, secure future. **Prosperity is suddenly defined as life itself** rather than in terms of life's possessions.

I Have Seen the Pain and Suffering, and I Cry Out to God, "Have Mercy!"

The life of privilege and opportunity is a distant, often faint hope, but it is actually possible for those who will endure the unparalleled hardship. For those of us who experience this horror, things will not be the same. Our true character will face a supreme test, and survival will depend on whether we turn our hearts to the Supreme Power, the One who gives life, the merciful, everlasting God and Father, the one and only blessed Hope.

I have seen the pain and suffering, and I cry out to God, "Have mercy!" Then in my heart I hear, "I am offering it even now, if only it will be received. I will not force My way into the lives of men. They can choose whom and what they will serve. They can eat the fruit of their ways or receive liberating truth and life-changing love." In prayer I ask, "Is it too late? Lord, please help us." **I pray for repentance, brokenness, and humility, for mercy received and mercy shared.** I hold on to God's promise "Blessed are the merciful, for they shall receive mercy."

I pray, "God, break our hearts by the power of Your Word and the love revealed through the cross of Christ. Break our stubborn will. Humble us that we may be mightily exalted as we exalt You and build our lives and future on Your rock-solid principles."

Only **right** relationships with God will produce the necessary resolve to fight the **right** fight in the **right** way. It is only through commitment to godly principles that we will have the character to make the sacrifices necessary to protect and preserve the truly priceless aspects of life. It becomes increasingly difficult to hear transforming truth when much of the mass media and entertainment community blatantly mock truth, promote twisted lifestyles, and assail traditional family values.

I am grateful that for the moment we have some national leaders who acknowledge the importance of prayer and faith. It is critically important that all believers pray for those in authority, because they must have the resolve and wisdom from above in order to make and stand by correct decisions. As we pray, we must remember that no political leader or party can be seen as our hope and security apart from the guidance of Divine Providence.

We Will Bow Before God or Be Broken Before God

The only way we will miss the agony I have seen is by supernatural intervention—by God giving us wisdom, granting us clear communication between all concerned parties, and enabling us to uncover sinister plots. I believe with all my heart that we will bow before God or be broken before God. America cannot continue to rebel and choose darkness when, throughout our history, we have been exposed to so much light. I am not speaking of perfection or perfect hearts. I am pleading for all to sincerely seek to share life, to know love—God's love—and admit to the need for personal and public change. Real repentance will produce the necessary change in people's hearts and minds, which will result in a renewed national desire to protect all life, because life is precious.

Moved by Compassion and Unselfish Love

Our laws will begin to reflect the transformed hearts of voters and legislators guided by time-tested, proven principles. The family will once again be defined properly—husband, wife, and children. Our freedom will not only be diligently protected, but its benefits and blessings freely shared. While enjoying the privileges true prosperity affords us, we will cherish the responsibility and joy of sharing what we have with others. We will not be manipulated or motivated by greed, but moved by compassion and unselfish love.

A major part of the entertainment community will forsake the promotion of indulgent and perverse lifestyles and seek to inspire us to rise above our natural, depraved tendencies. Their tremendous ability will be used to present great and admirable acts as was Steven Spielberg's through *Schindler's List.* They will use their great talent to present people and stories worthy of respect rather than people committed to decadence. Let me make it clear: caring people will no longer be merely cursing the darkness. As surely as light dispels darkness, when the light begins to shine freely, its effect will be visible and undeniable. History confirms the need to defend the Christian faith, but in this day it will be the demonstration of faith's transforming power that inspires repentance and change.

I invite all who bear witness of the concern I have shared to join me in prayer, in pursuing the God of holiness, and in reaching out to others to share our blessings, great or small. Let's discover that the "joy of the Lord" is indeed our strength and hope.

A Call to Prayer

Please pray and share this message as God leads, while encouraging others also to join in prayer. Consider reading this message again each week and praying daily concerning the issues addressed. Let's pray . . .

- For all to bow before God in humility and not to wait to fall before Him in humiliation.

- For all in authority to have wisdom to make the right decisions and the resolve to stand by them.

- For the family of faith and all who love freedom to search their own hearts and turn from evil.

- For our enemies to be turned from deadly intent and acts and for their plans and deceptive practices to be exposed, thereby nullifying their actions and protecting the innocent.

- For the ultimate defeat of all terrorist activities.

- For peace in our hearts and on earth.

- For America and the free world not only to enjoy the fruit of prosperity, but also to compassionately and consistently share their blessings with others.

- For the Christian church family to live in oneness with God and in the unity of the Spirit that Jesus prayed for, so the world will know we are truly His disciples and He will be revealed through us as the ever-living Lord of all.

Is Comfort the Right Standard?

AMERICA IS accustomed to comfort. Russian-exiled prisoner Aleksandr Solzhenitsyn commented in the late 1970s that America was soft because the people were spoiled. He questioned whether we would have the moral resolve to stand up to the atheistic "evil empire" of the Soviets as it threatened world peace. Fortunately, we elected a strong president in 1980 who actively opposed the communists and ended decades of oppression for millions of people.

Today we face similar challenges. It is possible that terrorism will not be the ultimate culprit should the West collapse. Our real Achilles' heel may very well be the idolization of comfort. By this, I do not mean comfort in the sense of bringing peace of mind to those in distress. Scriptures refer to the Holy Spirit as the Comforter, so there is certainly nothing wrong with comfort in the bibilical sense.

No, I am referring to comfort as the material substitute for conviction, a worldly opiate providing a false sense of security. Many Americans look to possessions, privilege, and leisure for comfort. We measure success by the state of the economy. We judge political parties and elected officials by whether they improve our economic status. We bow to the throne of the almighty dollar.

But terrorism endangers our economy. Rising gas prices threaten our pocketbooks. Illegal immigration raises questions about our security. If our standard is comfort, then we are in trouble.

I am convinced that pressure will strengthen our character. If it takes economic pressure to get our attention—to get us to become one nation under God, with His principles guiding our lives and our future—then it will likely happen. If we insist on making material gain our god, on having no regard for moral values as long as we are financially strong, then our future is bleak.

God has blessed America and, as a result, her people have prospered. More than any other nation in history, we are uniquely positioned in the world to alleviate suffering and help those in need. America—her people, corporations, and government—has improved the lives of billions of people by promoting human rights, free trade, and humanitarian aid beyond our own borders. America consistently provides positive political, moral, and economic leadership.

Yet at the same time a dark underside thrives. Drug abuse creates a worldwide black market for narcotics, spawning crimes beyond substance abuse. The back alleys of Hollywood produce pornographic material that eats away at healthy relationships. Greedy companies exploit cheap labor, trapping hard-working people in poverty. High-powered, well-funded lobbyists buy influence in the halls of legislation.

At the center of America's paradox of blessing and exploitation lies a culture war whose winner will mold the America that must respond to the pressures of tomorrow.

We must come to understand that morals have more value than money. People are more important than profits. Are we a nation controlled by lust for material gain or a people compelled to help those in need? Are we marked by our immoral passions or by our compassionate giving?

If it takes the loss of material comfort to reshape our thinking and compel us to return to absolute principles, then perhaps that day is coming—and maybe very soon. We should not wait for God to bring such judgment upon us. Our nation's character must be strengthened to withstand the pressures that await us. That strength will only come with a change of heart, a change of mind, and a change of measure.

Read 1 John 2:15–17.

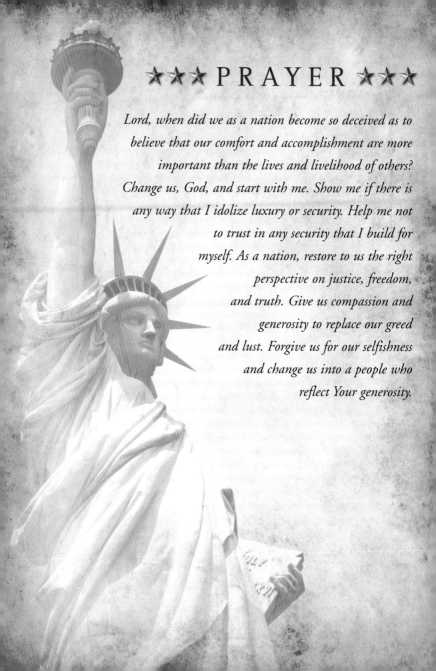

★★★ PRAYER ★★★

Lord, when did we as a nation become so deceived as to believe that our comfort and accomplishment are more important than the lives and livelihood of others? Change us, God, and start with me. Show me if there is any way that I idolize luxury or security. Help me not to trust in any security that I build for myself. As a nation, restore to us the right perspective on justice, freedom, and truth. Give us compassion and generosity to replace our greed and lust. Forgive us for our selfishness and change us into a people who reflect Your generosity.

The Morality of Stem Cell Research

STEM CELL RESEARCH continues to play a key role in political debates. Arguments supporting the research raise many questions about the various forms of stem cell research and force us to examine our own attitudes toward this evolving science.

As Christians, should we support or oppose stem cell research? Can it deliver on its promise to cure debilitating diseases? Is it akin to human experimentation? These questions must be answered in order to avoid purely emotional reactions to a highly sensitive subject.

Scientists are still discovering new facts about stem cells, but the general belief is that stem cells can transform into virtually any other type of cell, like a brain cell, blood cell, or muscle cell. These new cells can then replace damaged cells in the human body, thereby leading to healing for a wide range of diseases.

Scientists primarily work with two kinds of stem cells from animals and humans: embryonic and adult. There is little moral debate about harvesting adult stem cells, so more progress has been made in this area than in others. Research shows that stem cells taken from your own body are more likely to create healthy cells for your own use. Stem cells from other people run a higher risk of being rejected by your body.

The moral debate surrounds the use of embryonic stem cells, which can be taken from fertilized human embryos often used for in vitro fertilization. The root issue is whether a fertilized egg constitutes a human life. It is the same issue that determines the morality of abortion. That is, if human life begins at conception, abortion and embryonic stem cell research result in the destruction of a human life.

However, if life begins at a later stage, such as the beginning of brain wave activity (about forty days after conception), then embryos could be considered usable human tissue. The difficulty with this position is the fact that embryos undeniably contain the potential to become a human life. Many "snowflake children" are alive today, deriving life from the very embryos that scientists wish to use for stem cell research.

President Bush and many elected officials have refused to federally fund research on embryonic stem cell research. Privately, the research continues, but at this point your tax dollars are not being used to destroy human embryos.

Pro-abortionists cannot allow debate on the beginning of life because it threatens their fundamental commitment to abortion on demand. If embryonic stem cell research proves immoral, then abortion logically becomes inexcusable as well.

Research on adult stem cells continues unabated. Republicans and Democrats both support and fund this research. Everyone wants to find a cure for Parkinson's disease, muscular dystrophy, leukemia, and all of the other potentially affected ailments. But some people do not want to sacrifice human lives to achieve that end. There is no evidence to show that finding these cures depends on the destruction of embryos.

In politics and in much of the media, nobody seems willing to discuss the real issue, which is when life begins. Each of us must decide what is important in this debate. Does life begin at conception or at another point? Are human embryos worthy of protection? We all want to see Michael J. Fox get well, but not if it requires the involuntary sacrifice of another person's life.

Read Jeremiah 1:5 and Isaiah 53:5.

★★★ PRAYER ★★★

Father, we ask that in Your mercy and grace You send us cures for devastating diseases like Parkinson's and leukemia. If it breaks our hearts so much to see people suffering, we know it breaks Your heart even more. Give scientists wisdom and resources to discover Your solution to these illnesses. Please turn our nation away from the dangerous direction we now travel, away from stem cell research. Open our eyes to this gross injustice to the unborn. Do not allow us to elevate our own lives above those You have created and already have a future planned for. Defend the defenseless and use us, Your children, to be their voices. Bring healing as only You can, but do not allow our nation to devalue life You have created.

Speaking of Religion and Politics

NEARLY THIRTY YEARS AGO I was kicked off television for exercising my First Amendment right: freedom of speech. The local ABC affiliate received some angry phone calls after, as a minister, I dared to say that the Bible calls homosexuality a sin.

My opinion that gay sex is unnatural, destructive to society, and potentially dangerous to one's health had, in their estimation, put them in bad light. At the time, the so-called Fairness Doctrine prescribed equal time for opposing views. The station determined that forty seconds of my opinion needed balancing. Therefore, my entire half-hour time slot was forfeited and given to promote sexuality. Half an hour to balance forty seconds—government "fairness" at work!

In response to a strong public outcry, the station's decision was overturned, and we were put back on the air. Within a short time, the Fairness Doctrine was also discarded because it was found to be in a bad light to broadcast and station owners.

A quarter of a century later, religious leaders and institutions continue to operate under a virtual gag order. While faithful ministries work to build the family, strengthen marriages, rebuild lives, feed the hungry, clothe the naked, give water to the thirsty, provide shelter for the homeless, and engage in other activities contributing to a functional society, many work under the intense scrutiny of the IRS.

As soon as spiritual leaders speak out too much on issues they believe are important—issues that could have a political impact, such as gay marriage, abortion, judicial activism, mercy killing, and other matters rooted in morality—they face potential tax ramifications. These tax revisions would gut their humanitarian relief efforts and effective ministry outreaches by revoking their non-profit status.

When James Dobson's Family Research Council organized "Justice Sunday," the media and Capitol Hill did not respond positively. Clearly, the event was a partisan Republican effort to mobilize people of faith to impact the political process. In this case, it was to pressure Congress to actually vote for or against President Bush's judicial nominees. Many people did not like this.

It reminds me of the early 1960s when those meddling preachers wouldn't shut up about racism. The Southern Democrats fought hard to keep religious activists in their place, but to no avail. Those church rallies eventually got completely out of hand and led to the civil rights movement. (It is interesting to note that in the South, Democrat senators voted 21-1 against the Civil Rights Act of 1964. One of the few Republicans voting against the act was Senator Barry Goldwater of Arizona, who asserted, "You can't legislate morality.")

Paul Greenberg, editorial editor for the *Arkansas Democrat-Gazette*, defended Christians' right to engage in political dialogue: "The moral imagination of Americans, which is so much a part of our national character, is inseparable from our religious roots."

The church and people of our faith must continue to stand up for moral issues. We should not become "kingmakers" or the pawn of political parties, but we must remain active in the political process. We must use our voices to engage in social debate and our votes to impact the political process. To refrain from doing so would not only be un-American but also, in fact, un-Christian.

Read Romans 13:1–7.

★★★ PRAYER ★★★

Lord, it is so easy to take the attitude of "an eye for an eye."
Christians in our nation are regularly silenced and punished when
standing up for Your moral standards. Our natural reaction is to want
to withdraw or retaliate, but Your Word tells us to respond differently.
Help me to obey You when You tell me to honor my government and to
respect its laws. Convict me to get involved in the political process so
that I am not part of the problem, but part of the solution. Vindicate
Your people when it comes to fairness in the media and bureaucratic
persecution. Help us to commit to follow Your path, fight
our battles, and restore our nation.

What Is Freedom?

THE CONCEPT OF FREEDOM is one that most Americans would claim to comprehend. But after generations of living free, do we really understand what would be lost if just a piece of our freedom were taken away?

Remember the days just after September 11, 2001? The airlines were shut down and air travel suffered for months. Professional football games were postponed. Large events were canceled. The security measures implemented since then have cost billions of dollars and demanded countless hours of work.

Imagine what life would be like if we suffered a barrage of suicide bombers, truck bombs, and armed assaults similar to what happens in place like Iraq and Israel.

Would there be a Super Bowl? Would fans be willing to risk their lives and the lives of their children to go to a Home Run Derby? Football, hockey, basketball, auto racing, and all other sporting events that draw large crowds are still potentially high-risk targets.

In Israel, even a night out on the town can be deadly. Suicide bombers walk into supermarkets and restaurants, detonating themselves and murdering anyone standing nearby. If this type of horror plagued American cities, life would be completely different. We don't think twice about going to the mall and casually shopping for hours. We routinely eat out, never considering which restaurants might be safer than others. For us, they are all safe. We have not lost that freedom.

Every day millions of Americans board airplanes, trains, and buses to travel for business or leisure. Public transportation continues to run as normal. Someone riding the subway probably worries more about getting mugged than bombed. Our freedom to move about has not been damaged.

Recently, I drove through Rocky Mountain National Park in Colorado. My wife and I admired the majesty of the Continental Divide. We photographed elk and sheep in their natural environment. Never once did we worry about terrorism. Yet I could not help but wonder what life would be like if we were not winning this war on terror. Would we be able to enjoy our national parks, beaches, or public places?

The greedy, deceptive practices of Enron that cost employees their investments and retirement funds pale in comparison to what terrorists want to do to our economy. They don't want to destroy our potential to care for our futures; they want to destroy our very opportunity to have a future. Peace and the potential for prosperity are among freedom's greatest gifts, and we must fight to protect them.

An old saying warns that you don't know what you have until it is gone. Truly, we take so much for granted in this country that it is easy to lose sight of how much is at stake. We must not allow terrorists to shut us down and isolate us from the rest of the world. As President Kennedy said years ago, "Let every nation know, whether it wishes us well or ill, that we shall pay any price, bear any burden, meet any hardship, support any friend, oppose any foe, in order to assure the survival and the success of liberty."

President Bush has staked his reputation on his efforts to defend our way of life. Our soldiers are risking (and some are losing) their lives to protect our freedom. The rest of us must do our part to secure the future for our children and grandchildren not only for the sake of our loved ones, but also for the sake of freedom.

Read Psalm 100.

★★★ PRAYER ★★★

Thank You, Lord, for the freedom we enjoy in this country.
You have blessed us beyond what we deserve. Thank You for
the gifts of transportation, recreation, financial security, and so much
more. We are all guilty of taking Your blessings for granted. Remind
us continually of how You protect us and cause us to prosper. Help us
not to squander the freedom You have bestowed upon us.
Help us protect it as the treasure that it is.

The Enemy Within

"THESE ARE THE TIMES that try men's souls," wrote Thomas Paine in *The Crisis* as America stood on the brink of war in 1776. More than three centuries later, we face another crisis.

Accusation abounds in our world. America is called the "Great Satan." Our president is called a liar and warmonger. Conservatives are called racists and bigots. Christians are called hypocrites and zealots.

As a conservative, a Christian, and an American, I am sensitive to these accusations. When most of the accusations are outright lies, I am naturally defensive.

Throughout my lifetime, however, I have learned that in order to avoid becoming any of these terrible things, I must sometimes listen to the accusations and search them for any grain of truth. Enemies will occasionally tell me the truth, though they do so with a harsh, judgmental spirit.

I was once criticized and characterized by the media as an "angry preacher." For many years, I dismissed the criticism, claiming my anger to be righteous indignation. It wasn't until later that I recognized that part of my anger was leveled against my own tormenting temptations and failure to practice what I preached. I was given to appetites and desires with a self-centeredness that was unbecoming and very un-Christlike. When I began to love my enemies, I discovered that they could be very effective teachers.

Americans often criticize Muslims for oppressing women, citing the requirement that they wear the burkha, a head-to-toe covering that keeps them from revealing any sinful flesh. Yet in the West we have traded the burkha for the bikini. The East tried to get women to cover up, while the West tries to get them to uncover. One side demands modesty while the other side "defends women's rights." They accuse us of being immoral while we accuse them of being intolerant. The result is a clash of civilizations. Somewhere in between lies self-respect, but neither side wants to listen to its enemies.

The West gasps in horror at the shedding of innocent blood, whether it's at the hands of misdirected gunfire or suicide bombers. Yet we allow babies who could otherwise lead normal, healthy lives to be terminated in the womb at any point up until birth.

We call our decadence "freedom of expression" and our indulgence "freedom of choice" when in reality many people are slaves to their own compulsions and desires, held captive by their sensual appetites.

"Your conduct is an invitation to the enemy," Paine wrote to those who were closest to the battle. We would be wise to examine our own conduct to ensure what we are not giving our enemies any legitimate justification to war against us and rally support around the world.

History confirms the importance of recognizing evil, standing firmly against it, and fighting it when necessary. Still, we must consider whether the accusations of our present-day enemies could guide us to examine our own hearts. Let's seek to make certain that accusations of greed, immorality, and self-centeredness are not accurate.

While we must not lose the resolve to resist those who seek to kill us, we should also resolve to do some personal soul-searching to examine our hearts and actions. We can easily see the enemy coming at us from the outside, but to survive the current crisis, we must learn to identify and overcome the enemy within.

Read Jeremiah 17:9–10 and Psalm 139:23–24.

★★★ PRAYER ★★★

Lord, how humbling to think that our enemies might have valid reasons to criticize us. As a Christian nation, we should be a city on a hill, shining truth and goodness for the world to see, but instead we have allowed darkness to creep in. Search us, O God, and see if there is any wickedness in us. Cleanse us of sins, both secret and public. Give us a blameless testimony before our enemies. When they look at our lives, may they see lifestyles that match our claimed convictions. Let our light so shine before them they will see our good works and turn to glorify You. Make us meek and gentle, willing to accept the correction of others and Your Spirit so that we can overcome the enemy within.

Reclaiming the Spirit of September 12

SEPTEMBER 2001: After suffering shocking and devastating terrorist attacks on the U.S. mainland, America became a changed nation. Rescue workers became acclaimed heroes. Inspirational stories of ordinary citizens engaged in extraordinary acts of compassion for their fellow countrymen emerged across the land.

Members of Congress, both Democratic and Republican alike, stood shoulder-to-shoulder on the steps of the Capitol singing "God Bless America." Leaders of the House and Senate came together and passed a resolution that "thanks those foreign leaders and individuals who have expressed solidarity with the United States" and "asks them to continue to stand with the United States in the war against international terrorism." The same resolution committed to support "increased resources in the war to eradicate terrorism" and "the determination of the president…to bring to justice and punish the perpetrators of these attacks as well as their sponsors."

In the days following the attacks, America woke up to the evil that exists—the face of terror that seeks to kill innocent people, steal peace and prosperity, and destroy the very way of life that freedom has given us. We sensed that something greater than mankind was at work, and we resolved to be on the right side of the struggle. We discovered compassion for our neighbors that we never knew existed. And we realized that our trivial disagreements and petty arguments amounted to nothing compared to the concerns of our world.

Fast-forward two years later to September 2003: Two murderous regimes had fallen. For millions of oppressed people, the opportunity to live in a free society had arrived. The two architects of these regimes—Saddam Hussein and Osama bin Laden—remained at large, but as is the case with all fugitives, their days were numbered. Other countries were rooting out, sometimes by force, the cancerous cells of terror attempting to metastasize within their borders. Only a few rogue nations and groups continued to threaten the lives of Americans and the peace of the world.

Yet inside our own country a strange phenomenon was happening. The court's greatest recent victory was to remove the Ten Commandments from a public place. Hollywood's brightest stars were calling America "a dumb puppy that has big teeth that can bite and hurt you" and telling prospective coalition members, "We [America] can't beat anyone anymore." Presidential hopefuls unashamedly told the American people that their commander-in-chief lied to them in order to bring war upon an undeserving dictatorship. Greedy lawyers pursued lawsuits against our top airlines, the New York Port Authority, and others who suffered great losses in the attacks.

Somewhere we lost the spirit of America—the spirit of post 9/11 that compelled us to put the needs of others above our own, the spirit that taught us that evil must be recognized, the spirit that convicts us we were the good guys, the spirit that assured us we would win the war on terror.

On September 12, 2001, we came together. But since that day, too many Americans have chosen the path of cynicism, selfishness, and ignorance. Once again America must wake up to the truths that seemed so clear in the wake of tragedy: people matter most; evil exists and must be overcome; we must stand together, or we will fall apart.

When freedom is attacked, our resolve to pay whatever price necessary to protect it must deepen, and selfishness must be forsaken to make the necessary sacrifices.

Read Philippians 2:1–4.

★★★ PRAYER ★★★

Father, how quickly we forgot what You taught us in the midst of trial and tribulation. The horrors of September 11 devastated us, but You brought good from it by uniting us in service and love for one another. Forgive us, Lord, for turning our backs on this blessing. Your Son gave us the perfect example of selfless sacrifice when He came from heaven to die for us. Conform us into His image and teach us how to lay our lives down for others as He did. Remind us constantly of the price we must pay to protect the freedom You've blessed us with and give us the resolve to pay that price.

The Right to Retaliate

JESUS CHRIST was not a violent man. Even when unjustly taken before the Roman court, He did not defend Himself. Instead, He allowed them to crucify Him for crimes He did not commit. If we are to follow His example, should we feel justified when America goes after evil dictators? How can President Bush, who openly professes Christianity, defend Israel's retaliatory strikes in the Palestinian territories and Syria?

These are tough questions. Most Christians and most Americans believe in self-defense, but when we extend that right to "pre-emptive" actions on foreign soil, the justification becomes less convincing. Though we believe it is necessary, we don't always know how to reconcile our Christianity with our gut feeling.

Two biblical examples provide insight into the nature of God, and their lessons bolster America's confidence in her fight against evil. The first is the familiar story of David and Goliath (1 Samuel 17).

The Philistine army was marching across the land, terrorizing and slaughtering innocent people. At the battlefront, Goliath defied God's followers and demanded a fight. The people were terrified. But God sent David to meet the enemy and kill him. David did not negotiate, and he did not wait for Goliath to enter his hometown. Instead, he met the giant in his territory, knocked him down and cut off his head!

Modern similarities to this story are startling. Bands of murderers are pursuing God's followers and others who hold freedom dear. There is only one country fully capable and willing to face this enemy. So America is meeting the enemies where they stand (or hide), stopping them, capturing them, and, when necessary, destroying them.

The other biblical example is found in the New Testament in the form of a parable told by Jesus Himself (Matthew 18:23–35). There was a king who wanted to settle the accounts of his servants. One servant could not pay his debt and begged the king for mercy. The king took pity on the servant, canceled the obligation, and let him go.

When that servant went out, he found one of his fellow servants who owed him money. The fellow servant begged for mercy, but the first servant had the man thrown into prison until he could pay the debt. When the king heard of what had happened, he called the first servant in, berated him for his lack of mercy and turned him over to the jailers, who tortured him until he paid everything back.

The story ends with Jesus saying, "My heavenly Father will also do the same to you, if each of you does not forgive his brother from your heart" (v. 35).

Here we see both forgiveness and vengeance. Jesus' sacrifice for us provides the ultimate forgiveness. But for those who do not forgive others, there is only the wrath of God. Indeed, many Arabs have no forgiveness for perceived debts on the part of America and their ancestral brothers in Israel.

Interestingly, the king did not punish the wicked servant directly. He had his governmental staff torture the man. Today, God does not strike down individuals where they stand. Instead, He allows our governmental military institutions to carry out vengeance on those who terrorize.

For decades now, America and the rest of the world have pursued a path of mercy and peace, but some refuse to follow. As long as the enemy targets the innocent—whether at the World Trade Center or at a Haifa restaurant—America will continue to support retaliation against those who partake in these crimes, regardless of their location.

Read 1 Samuel 17.

★★★ PRAYER ★★★

Father, since the beginning of time, You have stood strong on behalf of Your children. Whether You have led them in the battle or they have defended themselves against attack, You have given victory time and again. Because You are holy and perfect, because You alone have pure motives, only You can decide when a war is just. We seek to follow You alone when faced with decisions about international conflict. When freedom is threatened and the innocent are oppressed, use America, the nation You have blessed, to restore peace and liberty. Help us to forgive those who have wronged us so that we can continue to receive Your grace.

One Nation
Indivisible

ELECTION SEASON always brings back a recycled theme: the tale of two Americas. Granted, dividing people into groups is not unique to politics. We split ourselves into male and female, black and white, old and young, rich and poor, straight and gay, Christian and non-Christian, urban and rural, Republican and Democrat, immigrant and native, and countless other categories.

The old divide-and-conquer technique has been around for ages. But while politicians try to tear us apart, the truth is that when it comes to the most important issues of the day, we are all in this together. We can call ourselves whatever we want, but to the rest of the world, we are simply Americans.

Despite the dozens of nations represented by the victims killed in the World Trade Center, America was the target on September 11. The terrorists did not check the passports of those on the United and American Airline flights and dismiss the Arabs on board. They did not evacuate the Pentagon of any Muslim servicemen or women. Their destruction was focused on anyone in their way as they attacked the one country they have labeled the "Great Satan."

When we entered into war to destroy the hornet's nests of terrorism—both in Afghanistan and Iraq—we went in not as two Americas but as one nation united against oppressive regimes.

The Al-Qaeda operatives who are brutally hacking Americans to death in Iraq and Saudi Arabia have yet to ask their victims if they are liberal or conservative. The politics of death seek only to maim and kill. Even when our enemy is holding citizens of other nations hostage, their target is still one America.

Those allied with America against the worldwide network of terrorists and, conversely, those opposed to our efforts do not differentiate between the red states and the blue states. Countries like England and Australia stand with the United States based on principle. At the other end of the spectrum, nations like Syria and Iran would continue to oppose America's policies even if another political administration took power, because they lack the moral clarity to know evil even when it festers within their very borders.

When Benjamin Franklin signed the Declaration of Independence, effectively putting his life and the lives of his loved ones on the line by standing up for freedom, he said, "We must all hang together, or assuredly we shall all hang separately."[1]

Those words still ring true as we stand up for freedom around the world. Despite attempts to divide us along a myriad of social, racial, political, and economic lines, we must realize that, as Americans, we have no choice but to stand together or we will surely fall apart.

Read Matthew 12:25.

★★★ PRAYER ★★★

God, division plagues this nation. We spend more time tearing one another down than building one another up. With every war, debate, and issue, we take sides and argue our priority responses instead of seeking proper compromise to establish good for the country. As long as Satan has us fighting among ourselves, we will not make progress for Your kingdom. Unite our hearts for the sake of Your good. Give us common goals and teach us to work together in harmony. For those of us who are Your children, make us examples of love and use us to bring this nation to a place where we can be used for Your purposes. Do not let division topple us, but instead make us one so that we can take Your light to a world in darkness.

Terminating the Republican Right

POLITICAL GURU Dick Morris has seen the future of the Republican Party and it is Austrian. The reason Arnold Schwarzenegger won the office of governor in California, Morris asserted on FOX's *Hannity & Colmes,* is because he is conservative on financial issues but liberal on moral issues. In other words, lower taxes and less spending combined with homosexual marriage, abortion on demand, strident environmentalism, and excessive gun control. Morris insists this model is the only way for the Republican Party to continue to exist as a major political force.

Is Arnold just an aberration on the electoral map, or is it the end of days for the Reagan-era marriage of family values and limited government?

Americans in general tend to adopt a "live and let live" philosophy. Certainly, there are a few moral police in pulpits—and the media loves to focus on them—but for the most part this country was built on the idea that all men and women are free to pursue happiness however they wish. After all, even our Creator put us on earth with guidelines for right and wrong and left the choice up to us. It is God's nature to let us choose our own path. At the same time, it is an irrefutable fact that our choices have obvious and undeniable consequences.

The pendulum of thought has swung from right to left over the last forty years. The societal pressures of my generation were strongly against divorce, abortion, homosexuality, and other historically aberrant or undesirable behavior. Perhaps my generation was too strong and insensitive, some may argue, and rightly so. For example, the church typically shunned the young woman who became pregnant and kept her hidden from the public eye. Or the man struggling with homosexual desires was ridiculed or physically assaulted instead of counseled or otherwise helped. Society, attempting to right a wrong, has gradually shifted away from this overzealous, hypocritical standard.

Now society is at a tipping point. The pendulum has swung so far to the left that politicians, judges, and the media are invading people's lives again, telling us to change our sacred religious institutions such as marriage and family, and pressuring us to accept things like promiscuity and homosexuality as norms, even in our children's public schools.

It is one thing to say, "I'm going to do whatever I want in my bedroom." It's another to say, "What we do in the bedroom is the same thing as what you do." It is fine to say, "We want to teach our kids whatever we wish," but it is beyond offensive to say, "We are going to teach your children that it is acceptable to have sex with anyone and everyone—and here's a condom!" It is perfectly understandable to say, "It's my body, I can do with it as I wish," but it is incomprehensible to say, "It's not a real human being inside of me, so I can kill it if it pleases me."

Here, Dick Morris fails to see that society is clearly swinging back the other way. The '60s generation said, "You're not going to tell us how to think!" Now many of those same people are trying to tell us how to think.

The Republican Party—and any other party for that matter—cannot afford to cast off all principles. If we forsake the unshakable absolutes that made this country strong, then the freedom and comfort we have known will soon be gone. Our future success will not come from eradicating the moralists but from embracing the morals.

Read Joshua 24:14–18.

★★★ PRAYER ★★★

God, You set a standard of holiness for us in Your Word that includes a respect for life, marriage, family, and freedom. Those of us in America who love and follow You want to keep these values central to our society. But there is a strong pull on us to abandon morality and embrace depravity. Lord, keep our hearts strong as we resist the constant pressure. Allow us to be a light to those choosing darkness. Do not let us be led astray by the voices of worldly logic. Hold us true to Your path.

Let Them March

HUNDREDS OF THOUSANDS of people, mostly women, continue to march in Washington, D.C., for abortion rights. The usual politicians and celebrities appear, chanting the same chants and waving the same banners. But behind their routine demonstrations and rhetoric is an undercurrent of panic.

The abortion movement is losing ground. In the last few years, they have been forced to take uncomfortable positions on important issues. They have come out in strong support of partial-birth abortion, a horrific procedure reminiscent of Nazi Germany. They oppose the Unborn Victims of Violence Act, also known as Laci and Conner's law, which puts them in a position that is decidedly harmful to women. And the major organizers of abortion rallies, such as the ACLU and NOW, have been defending women whose newborn babies suffered or died because of their mothers' drug abuse. In a country where only 17 percent of the population favors unfettered abortion on demand,[1] these positions are clearly out of step with general public.

Consider further the mixed message coming out of the American left as related to the war on terror. Despite the hornet's nest of terrorists, dictators, and murderous thugs tormenting the population in much of the Middle East, many celebrities continuously call for an end to aggression against "innocent women and children." Several even went through the efforts and expense to travel to Afghanistan and Iraq as human shields. Yet these very same people refuse to shield the most innocent among our own society—the unborn. This is the height of hypocrisy to defend the demented, dangerous and deadly while marching to kill the most helpless of all the innocents.

In a world where children are routinely born prematurely, late-term abortion has become more distasteful and unpopular. This is precisely why recent women's rights rallies are reported in many news sources as being about "reproductive rights and contraceptive use." Last time I checked, there was no mass movement against birth control! The core abortionists know that they are on the losing side, so they attempt to expand their stage.

Hillary Clinton summed it up well when she said from a rally podium, "If all we do is march today, that will not change the direction this country is headed under this administration."[2] Blatant political partisanship aside, she has a point. The radical left can protest all they want, but as the hearts and minds of Americans change, so will the social and political climate.

One very poignant quote came from a young girl who said, "If it weren't for choice, I would have a child."[3] One might speculate that she was raped, the child was grossly deformed, or her life was at risk. But her only reasoning was "I didn't want to bring a child into the world." So she killed it.

Americans do not approve of abortion as birth control. They do not like unnecessary killing. Education and technology now give prospective mothers the power to understand their choices, and more mothers are choosing life.

The pro-life movement must strive to teach women about their own bodies and the bodies in the womb. We must compassionately reach out to comfort those in difficult circumstances. We must speak the truth in love. Instead of cursing those who scream and shout in rallies across the country, we must pray for them and love them…even when they march.

Read Jeremiah 5:26–29.

★★★ PRAYER ★★★

Lord, for decades now our nation has failed to defend the needy and innocent. We have allowed millions to be brutally murdered, and we know this must infuriate You. There is blood on our hands, and we come asking for mercy and forgiveness. Thank You for the change that is taking place in the hearts of Americans. Thank You for the technology that has opened the eyes of so many to see the atrocity of abortion. Thank You for placing leaders over us who are determined to defend the weak and helpless in the womb. Protect the precious ones who have no voice or strength to protect themselves. Enable Your people to stand up for them as well. Continue to turn the tide of senseless murder in this country so that the life You create will be valued once again.

God Bless America?

FOR OVER 200 YEARS NOW, presidents, congressmen, and candidates have closed their speeches with three words: *God bless America!* Even when it could be construed as politically incorrect to invoke the name of God in a state setting, politicians from both major parties continue to do it. But can we really expect God to continually bless our country?

After two centuries of blessing and success, it seems that "God bless America" is not only our request but our testimony. I believe there is a direct connection between God's goodness and our historical respect for Him. Since the beginning, we as a nation have recognized and honored a Divine Being. Despite the wide range of religious beliefs, the importance of Providence in human affairs has rarely been denied.

Benjamin Franklin once said, "God governs the affairs of men. And if a sparrow cannot fall to the ground without His notice, is it probable that an empire can rise without His aid?"[1]

Americans, in general, have lived in accordance with Judeo-Christian values. Our country has proven to be compassionate, unselfish, and ready to assist those in need. When natural disaster strikes, whether an earthquake in Turkey or a famine in Sudan, America benevolently cares for the helpless and hurting. When tyrants from the Soviets to the Taliban try to oppress people, America works not to conquer but to liberate and grant the opportunity of freedom for all. Even our enemies in wartime, from the Germans in World War II to the Iraqis of today, have benefited from our generous rebuilding efforts, regardless of the time and money required.

America has, for the most part, set a positive example throughout the world—a city set on a hill. While the communists once built walls to keep people in, America consistently manages an influx of immigrants seeking the American Dream and all it offers.

At the same time, we must wonder if our contemporary pleas for God's blessings might be out of order. Our modern society often promotes practices, lifestyles, and ideas that run counter to the biblical principles of God.

Too many wealthy individuals and corporations are consumed by greed and dishonest practices. Too many politicians stir up envy among the poor. Those who "have" tend to horde it and those who "have not" hate those who do!

Sexual extremes and perversions have become commonplace among adults and children. Unhealthy addictions abound. Pop culture glorifies decadence and belittles morality. We fail to promote the importance of innocence and refuse to protect the defenseless unborn.

Our enemies hate the positive aspects of America, like freedom and opportunity, while exploiting the negative attributes. They use our sins to recruit pawns for their terror and justify their horrific actions. While we recognize the flawed thinking of the tormentors, Americans should analyze our own lives to make constructive changes, offset the criticism, and strengthen our country's foundation.

When floods occur in nature, the rising water often exposes the need to build on higher ground. Perhaps, as disaster strikes, it is time to go beyond merely asking God to bless America and begin to build our lives on higher moral ground.

Read Micah 6:8.

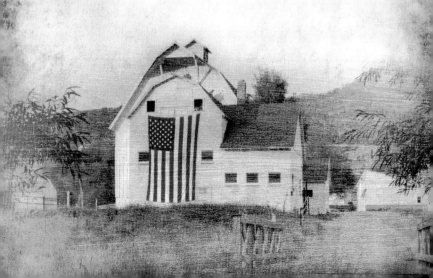

★★★ PRAYER ★★★

God, You have been gracious and kind to this country for so long. Thank You for Your goodness and faithfulness to us. Your Word tells us You bless those who obey You, but You resist the proud. Looking at our nation today, You must see immorality and arrogant pride as we reject Your ways for our own. We have no right to ask or expect Your blessing over us who are in such a state of rebellion. Change us Lord, from the inside out; begin with our hearts. Bring revival to this land so that we might seek You wholeheartedly as a society and respect Your ways. Teach us to live according to Your standards again. Return us to a place where we can again ask for Your blessing.

Who Will Change the World?

AMERICA IS in a constant state of change. Every two years the governing power can shift in one direction or another. But, on average, only half of the eligible voters in the country determine the course of their local, state, and national government.

We all know that our freedom is bought with a price. Many lives have been sacrificed to stave off the forces that seek to suppress our freedom of religion, expression, movement, and thought. In my lifetime alone, Nazis, communists, anarchists, and radical Muslims have sought to steal some of the most basic freedoms that Americans take for granted.

As evidenced by typical voter turnout, one of the most overlooked American freedoms is the right to vote. Going to the polls and filling out a ballot has the potential to influence the government that serves you. So many people around the world do not have this right and instead live under oppressive regimes that enslave them.

I believe it is not just an inherent right or a mere privilege to vote. I believe that voting is a duty, a concept that seems to be lost on the average American. As good stewards of freedom, we are obliged to care, stay informed, and be involved in the democratic process—even if it is only through the power of the vote.

Edward Everett Hale, former chaplain of the U. S. Senate, said, "I am only one—but I am one. I cannot do everything, but I still can do something." [1]

The most basic "something" is the vote. All citizens should get out and cast their votes on the issues that live beyond today and will affect our children and grandchildren. The issues facing us this year alone are momentous: national security, border control, abortion, gay marriage, education, and welfare.

Someone will determine how these things are handled. Someone will decide whether we should pursue terrorists and dictators with military aggression or engage in soft treaties and handshakes.

Someone will determine whether a child in a womb should be protected. Someone will decide whether tomorrow's schoolchildren will be taught that homosexuality is normal or even admirable.

Voters decide which leaders will chart the course of the free world. You can be assured that those with little regard for the principles that made us great will turn out in support of their very liberal ideals.

America will continue to make changes, but change does not begin at the ballot box. In a sense, that's where it ends. Real change begins when people decide that they care enough about their country to do something about it. Those who care enough to vote will be the agents of change. Will you be one of them?

The mass media seems committed to discouraging the voters who believe in moral and traditional family values. If you love God and country, do not be discouraged. Know that your vote influences this nation, and this nation influences the world. No one person is too insignificant to change the world. You can make a difference, and so can I.

Read 1 Peter 2:13–17.

★★★ PRAYER ★★★

God, I see that You have set governments and authorities in place in this world. Your Word tells us that the hearts of rulers are in Your hands. You are a God of order who works through men and systems to accomplish Your purposes. And You really want to use me as a part of that work. What a blessing it is to live in a country where my vote matters! Thank You for the privilege of taking part in a democratic system, and thank You for using Your children to direct the course of an entire nation. Convict my heart—and the hearts my bothers and sisters all over the country to get involved and stay involved in the political process. Give us Your eyes and heart to see issues and candidates as You see them. Show us Your path for America and help us to be responsible citizens in following Your steps.

A Matter of Life or Death

RELIGION CAN BE DANGEROUS. If you doubt it, just take a look at the "holiest" city in the world: Jerusalem. Sacred for thousands of years to three of the world's major religions—Judaism, Christianity, and Islam—this ancient city has been the focal point of wars, invasions, rebellions, terrorist attacks, crusades, persecutions, and occupations. Even today Jerusalem is a target for the guns of Hamas, the rockets of Hezbollah, and the suicide bombers of Palestine.

How can pious men, intent on pleasing God, live with such violence? How can a city of peace be surrounded by such hatred? The answer lies in mankind's concept of God and religion.

In the Torah, the God of the Old Testament declares: "I have set before you life and death, the blessing and the curse. So choose *life* in order that you may live…" (Deuteronomy 30:19, emphasis added).

This offer of life is reflected in the Christian New Testament when Jesus proclaimed: "The thief comes only to steal and kill and destroy; I came that they may have life, and have it abundantly" (John 10:10).

However, this emphasis on life does not translate to Islam, the third dominant religion in Jerusalem, at least not as preached by many Muslim leaders.

Hezbollah's Secretary General Hassan Nasrallah once proclaimed, "We have discovered how to hit the Jews where they are the most vulnerable. The Jews love life, so that is what we shall take away from them. We are going to win, because they love life and *we love death*" (emphasis added).[1]

The secretary general's comments are not isolated. Mufti Sheikh Ikrimeh Sabri, a cleric of the Palestinian Authority, said, "We tell [the world], in as much as you love life, *the Muslim loves death and martyrdom*"(emphasis added).[2]

So how do those who value life counter dangerous zealots who seek to destroy them? Politically, there is scriptural precedent to defend the innocent and punish evildoers. Iraqi Prime Minister Nouri al-Maliki told members of Congress that "Iraq will be the graveyard for terrorism."[3] This is not an insidious threat against mankind; it is a promise of hope and security to peaceful people. Governments have a responsibility to defend the defenseless from aggressive killers. Religious groups need not hinder such efforts to establish peace in areas of war.

But beyond political responsibility, the individual believer, both Christian and Jew, has three primary responses to the religion of death. First, we must return to the true essence of a relationship with God, which is found through repentance. As much as we despise the external evil that threatens us, we must shed the inner evil by turning from wickedness and wrongdoing.

Second, we must practice religion in its pure form, namely "to visit orphans and widows in their distress" (James 1:27). That is, we must serve our fellow man to relieve suffering. By reaching out to our neighbors and to those on the other side of the world, we demonstrate the love of God and express the religion of life.

Finally, we must pray. We who believe in the supernatural must remember that our "struggle is not against flesh and blood" (Ephesians 6:12). Our earthly enemies can only be defeated by heavenly forces, but they await our calling.

We are in the midst of a religious war. But we do not fight without hope because we know that victory is assured to those of us fighting on the right side. Have hope. The good guys will win. And in this case, the good guys are the ones on the side of life.

Read John 10:7–18.

★★★ PRAYER ★★★

Lord Jesus, You alone hold the power of life because You conquered death. I thank You that terror has no place in my heart because You are my Shepherd and Protector. Defend Your children in this world of war. Defend Your name against those who seek to defame it. Thank You for already laying down Your life for Your sheep. Now, complete the work of bringing in Your flock from the farthest reaches of the world. I ask that You make Your voice known to followers of Islam so that they too can find life in following You. Help me to respond to their threats with courage, love, and complete trust in Your victory.

Real Hope Lies in the Church

IN A DAY when politicians make promises of reform through their party and policies, we must remember one timeless truth: the true hope for America lies in the effectiveness of the local church.

The late Presbyterian pastor Clarence McCartney observed: "The poorest church building, a mere wooden shack, with broken windows and whining organ, and bare benches, and scattered worshippers and a dull preacher, is yet a far more significant part of any community or city than a library with its thousands of volumes, or a bank with its Grecian columns and its vaults busting with gold and silver."[1]

The church in America goes back to the foundation of our society. The Pilgrims left the religious persecution of their European homes to establish a new life in a land where they were free to worship as they chose. Thus, one of the first structures in early American towns was the church building, which stood not only as a place to worship but also to fellowship with neighbors, hold town activities, elect officials, and dispense local charity. Many of our great historical events and movements, from national independence to civil rights, have been located in or affiliated with churches.

Today, the local church still stands as a primary source of strength in communities from coast to coast, second only to the family. Whether it's an eighteenth-century cathedral in Boston or a converted shopping strip in South Central, Los Angeles, people in need still turn to the church.

Consider the wide range of aid and inspiration the church provides: fellowship with friends, consolation after the loss of a loved one, direction in difficult economic times, food for the poor, clothes for the needy, shelter for the homeless, and so much more. Churches whose members seek to live in harmony with New Testament teachings provide a secure and stable sense of family, an atmosphere of belonging, and evidence that there is a God who cares.

Governments may attempt to aid disadvantaged families and neighborhoods through financial assistance, but positive and permanent change seldom occurs simply by handing out cash grants. Without the personal touch of people who genuinely care about those in need, social welfare simply becomes a tax burden. But when finances are used to fuel the work of an existing core of concerned people, the positive effect is clearly demonstrated in the lives of those who are encouraged and enriched.

Archbishop William Temple wisely noted, "The church is the only society in the world which exists for the benefit of those outside its membership."[2]

This selfless service to the community can be contrasted with the cold, self-serving attitude sometimes seen in elected officials and bureaucratic government agencies. Government has a role in our lives, but its role is limited. When the church accepts its divinely-ordained role, there is no limit to the positive influence it can have in our lives and, in turn, our nation.

By empowering the local church to further its mission of helping their fellow man, we are empowering America to be strong. Through the power of the positive human touch, lives are being redeemed, families are being restored, and communities are being revitalized.

Read Acts 2:42–47.

★★★ PRAYER ★★★

Jesus, when You returned to the Father, You did not leave this world without hope. Instead, You left Your body, in the form of Your followers, to continue Your work. You told us that once You were gone, we would do greater works than You did. Now, as I look at this nation and the condition of our world, I am convinced that those greater works are needed more than ever. Equip Your church to be Your hands and feet in the streets, in homes, and in lives. Help us to follow Your example of compassion, acceptance, boldness and love as we seek to be a light in our communities. Completely transform lives, cities, our nation, and the world through Your church. Thank You for the privilege of representing You to the world. Make us into Your image so that the world can see You clearly.

Believers Must Fight on the Right Front

MANY CHRISTIANS are disturbed by recent trends against open expressions of Judeo-Christian principles. From the removal of Judge Moore's granite "Ten Commandments" monument in Alabama to the decision of activist judges in Massachusetts who seem eager to equate homosexual unions with traditional marriage, the forces of religious intolerance appear to be gaining ground. But this may not be the fight in which Christians wish to engage.

Christians around the world have suffered brutally for centuries from the Roman Empire to the Soviet Empire. Even today believers are being tortured, maimed, and killed for their faith. America still stands as a nation where people can worship how, when, and where they please.

It would be a national tragedy to tear down all of our national monuments that contain any religious reference or imagery. But even if the PC storm troopers tore down the statues of Moses in and on the Supreme Court in Washington, D.C., in the Library of Congress, and in the Ronald Reagan Building, they could not remove the legacy of the God of Moses from people's hearts. Even if the floor of the National Archives building were covered to conceal the Ten Commandments, the ears of our children would not be covered from hearing the principles contained in those simple instructions.

The windows of the U.S. Capitol could be shattered to eliminate the image of George Washington kneeling in prayer, but the power of prayer will continue to shatter the destructive forces in the lives of hurting people. The references to Almighty God could be cut out of all the speeches, writings, and monuments of Thomas Jefferson, Abraham Lincoln, and every other great American leader, but the influence of Almighty God will never be eliminated.

John Whitehead, president of The Rutherford Institute, recently wrote, "If Christians really want to have a positive impact on the world around them, let them return to their communities and tend to the sick, feed the poor, and stand for the weak and defenseless. Then maybe there will be no need for monuments."[1]

While it is tempting to join the fight over the symbols of our faith, the real battle is not on this front. The reason that our Founding Fathers wrote about God was because the truth of God was written on their hearts. Our forefathers' testimonies of faith should be preserved, but they will only represent a fading sentiment if these principles are not practiced by this present generation.

We must understand that the critical point is the power of our testimony now rather than our zealous attempts to protect the past. Our major concern should be living the Ten Commandments, not defending where they sit. "In God We Trust" inscribed on our coins is not as much of an issue as whether we trust God with all of our hearts. Reciting "one nation under God" in the pledge is not nearly as important as knowing that this nation must be under God's direction and protection. These are the real issues at hand.

Supporting the public display of the Ten Commandments, speaking your mind, and expressing your opinion are both your privileges and responsibilities as a citizen, and starting a movement to force the display of engraved stones will not change hearts. God says "not by might nor by power, but by My spirit." Spiritually, it is not muscle that wins; it is the power of prayer and the liberated life that prevails.

The real power to positively impact our country lies in the ability of us Christians to demonstrate the love of God in our lives, not to organize our ranks around courthouses. We don't need to discuss or debate the issue of prayer; we just need to pray. Praying, believing Christians are the most powerful force in the universe. Those inclined to rally the troops and engage in a fight should assume the rightful and powerful position of spiritual warriors—on their knees in prayer.

Read 2 Chronicles 7:14.

★★★ PRAYER ★★★

Father God, You told us that when we humble ourselves before You in prayer, seek Your face, and turn from our wicked ways, You will hear us from heaven and heal our land. So I come before You with a humble heart. Please teach me to seek Your face over everything else. Forgive me for turning from Your instructions and Your heart. Help me to be an instrument both in word and deed for Your glory, so that other Americans will see Your love shining through me. Hear my prayer, Father, and heal the heart of America. Teach me to seek and serve You in everything I do, so that I can be a light for You once again.

Endnotes

DAY 1

1. President George Washington's Inaugural Address to the U.S. Congress, April 30, 1789, New York.
2. Patrick Henry's speech to the House of Burgesses, May 1765, Virginia.
3. President Abraham Lincoln's Proclamation for a National Fast Day, March 30, 1863, Washington, D.C.
4. President Harry S. Truman to the Attorney General's Conference on Law 5. Enforcement Problems, February 15, 1950, Washington, D.C.
5. President Jimmy Carter's speech, March 1976.
6. President Ronald Reagan's speech, August 23, 1984, Dallas, Texas.

DAY 3

1. "The History of the National Day of Prayer" from the Web site of the National Day of Prayer Task Force, www.ndptf.org (2007).

DAY 4

1. *Inspiring Quotations: Contemporary & Classical,* compiled by Albert M. Wells Jr., Thomas Nelson Publishers, 1988.

DAY 5

1. Simon Wiesenthal, http://thinkexist.com/quotes/Simon_Wiesenthal/ (2007).

DAY 7

1. "The Hispanic Challenge" by Samuel P. Huntington from the Web site of Harvard University, http://cyber.law.harvard.edu/blogs/gems/culturalagency1/SamuelHuntingtonTheHispanicC.pdf (2007).

DAY 8

1. "Justice: A New Controversy in the Fetal-Rights Wars" by Sarah Childress, *Newsweek,* March 29, 2006.

DAY 10

1. "Amish grandfather: 'We must not think evil of this man,'" CNN.com, posted October 5, 2006, www.cnn.com (2007).
2. "Fifth girl dies after Amish school shooting," CNN.com, posted October 3, 2006, www.cnn.com (2007).
3. "Gotta Serve Somebody" by Bob Dylan from the album, *Slow Train Coming,* Columbia Records, 1979.

DAY 12

1. "A Model of Christian Charity," a discourse written by John Winthrop aboard the Arbella during the voyage to Massachusetts, 1630, from *Life and Letters of John Winthrop* by Robert C. Winthrop, 1867, Michigan Historical Reprint Series.
2. President John F. Kennedy's speech on the twentieth anniversary of the Voice of America, February 26, 1962, Washington, D.C.

DAY 13

1. *How to Win the Culture War: A Christian Battle Plan for a Society in Crisis* by Peter Kreeft, InterVarsity Press, 2002.

DAY 15
1. An interview with Staff Sgt. Mike McNaughton on WAFB-TV, Channel 9, Baton Rouge, Louisiana.

DAY 18
1. "The War on Religion" by Paul Greenberg, posted by permission April 26, 2005 on the *Jewish World Review*'s Web site, www.jewishworldreview.com/cols/greenberg042605.asp (2007).

DAY 19
1. President John F. Kennedy's Inaugural Address, January 20, 1961, Washington, D.C.

DAY 20
1. *The Crisis* by Thomas Paine, December 23, 1776, from a collection of essays written during the American Revolution.

DAY 21
1. The U.S. House of Representatives Joint Resolution 61, 107th Congress, September 12, 2001, Washington, D.C.
2. "Johnny Depp: 'U.S. is like a stupid puppy,'" CNN.com, posted September 3, 2003, regarding Johnny Depp's interview with Germany's *Stern* magazine, www.cnn.com (2007).

DAY 23
1. Benjamin Franklin's words upon signing the Declaration of Independence, July 4, 1776, Philadelphia.

DAY 25
1. The Gallup Poll Questionnaire Profile, October 24–27, 2003, www.gallup.com (2007).
2. "10 for Change Campaign Already Registering New Voters" by Katie Ijams, posted 2004, www.now.org/nnt/spring-2004/10.html (2007).
3. "Hundreds of thousands march on the National Mall," *Fort Worth Star-Telegram*, April 26, 2004.

DAY 26
1. Benjamin Franklin's speech to the Constitutional Convention, June 28, 1787, Philadelphia.

DAY 27
1. "Lend a Hand" by Edward Everett Hale from *Masterpieces of Religious Verse*, edited by James Dalton Morrison, Harper, 1948.

DAY 28
1,2. "Dealing in Death" by Steven Stalinsky, *National Review*, May 24, 2004.
3. Iraqi Prime Minister Nouri al-Maliki's speech to the U.S. Congress, July 26, 2006, Washington, D.C.

DAY 29
1. *Inspiring Quotations: Contemporary & Classical*, compiled by Albert M. Wells Jr., Thomas Nelson Publishers, 1988.
2. This quote is attributed to Archbishop of Canterbury William Temple, www.worldofquotes.com/author/William-Temple (2007).

DAY 30
1. "Judge Roy Moore Is Inheriting an Ill Wind" by John W. Whitehead (2003), http://www.rutherford.org/articles_db/commentary.asp?record_id=239 (2007).